DEDICATION

This book is dedicated to
Alan Rogers Lindquest
(1891–1984)
my teacher, my mentor, my friend.

Acknowledgments

The stories in this book describe lessons I've learned from the places I've sung. None of these encounters would have happened without the assistance and encouragement of some dear friends and supporters. Julie and Rig Dees were especially instrumental in nurturing my dream to perform. The men and women who have served on the Amerson Ministries board have embraced God's calling on my life and stood by me even in times when the future seemed uncertain. I am in their debt.

Thanks goes to my friend, Barbara Heimburger, for poking and prodding me on this project. It might not have happened without her. Our connection is another sign of God's grace. I also want to thank my friends Harry Langdon for outstanding cover photos and David Darrow for his superb front cover design.

Finally, my deep love and gratitude goes to my wife, Kristine and our family. Kristine has endured lots of nights with a husband on the road but never wavered in her support. Our children, Katherine and Matthew, have blessed us along with their spouses, David and Vanessa and five (at this writing) amazing grandsons, Hudson James Pennington, Judah Hayes Pennington, Theodore Allen Pennington, Ezra McCray Pennington and Walker Wesley Amerson. I pray these boys will someday read these stories about their Papa, find their voices, and become warriors for God's kingdom.

TABLE OF CONTENTS

INTRODUCTION

I have often been asked if I was born with this voice or if I took voice lessons. The answer is yes. God gave me a gift, and I have done my best to train my voice and make it all that it can be. Some people look enviously at those who have been given a talent. I believe that such a gift is a huge responsibility.

Even though I studied voice, I've always tried not to let my training get in the way of communicating with the audience. True classical *bel canto* singing focuses on vowels and learning to sing them properly. Some singers seem to glory in the sound of their voices and focus so much on vowels that it's hard to understand what they are singing. My approach is more conversational. If you can't understand the words, what's the point? People have often told me that they felt as if I were talking to them as I sang. I take that as a compliment.

As you read this book, I hope that you feel as though I'm talking with you and sharing some of the high notes of my singing career. This book tells stories of different places where I have sung and some of the things that I have learned along the way. As I recalled these stories, I found myself laughing and sometimes crying as I reminisced about meaningful musical moments.

My life has been blessed with opportunities to sing in some of the most marvelous settings in the world. May the tales of this troubadour allow God's grace to touch your life and may you use your gifts to bring joy to others to the glory of God. "This is my story. This is my song."

—Steve Amerson

PROLOGUE

The film, *Chariots of Fire*, depicts the story of Olympic runner, Eric Liddell, and his participation in the 1924 Paris Olympics. Liddell was a man of faith who took a stand and refused to run in the 100-metres event he had trained for because the competition was scheduled on a Sunday. The public and the press ridiculed him for holding firm to his belief of honoring the Sabbath. Instead, Liddell ran in the 400-metres race, an event for which he had not trained. He won the gold medal.

When asked about his commitment, Liddell said, "I believe that God made me for a purpose, but he also made me fast and when I run, I feel his pleasure."

This sentiment has stayed with me. When I'm in good voice, when the acoustics are right, and when the music fills my heart and my voice, I enjoy a feeling like no other. *When I sing, I feel God's pleasure.*

I hope that the stories in these pages will encourage you to find whatever it is that lets you feel God's pleasure.

CHAPTER ONE

Small Beginnings

"Do not despise these small beginnings, for the
LORD rejoices to see the work begin…"

— Zech. 4:10

"Steve, when did you know you could sing?" people often
ask.

"Almost from day one."

Growing up in a pastor's home meant that music would
be an inevitable part of my life. My mom played the piano,
and my brothers and I joked that my dad made a joyful noise.
Although Mom read music, she mostly played by ear. Since
she also led the children's choirs in the churches where my
dad pastored, it was pretty much a given that we three boys
would sing in the choir. We were Amersons—so we sang!

From time to time, my older brothers and I sang trios. Both
of my brothers had nice voices and could sing harmony by
ear, but I'm the only one who made music his career. To this
day, I constantly remind my brothers that "I am the younger,
more handsome, more talented, more humble brother." It's
become my mantra, and they roll their eyes at me whenever

they hear me say it. Several years ago, I met a friend of my brother Phil's at an event in Texas. He said, "Oh, you're the younger, more handsome, more talented brother." How could I disagree? My reputation had preceded me.

In our own ways, each of us has been involved in ministry of some sort. My brother, Phil, has been a pastor, a missionary, a professor and a seminary president.

My brother, Bill, was a teacher and high school principal and stayed involved in church lay-leadership by serving in various capacities at Wesley Chapel United Methodist Church in New Albany, Indiana, which is the church my father pastored when I was born.

As a testament to the love that the congregation had for my parents, when they retired in New Albany, Dad returned to the staff to work part time. For a pastor to return to the staff of a church in which he previously served is a rarity, but the congregation welcomed Mom and Dad back into the fold. Dad wound up burying some of the folks whom he led to the Lord and some of the couples whom he married.

With we three Amerson boys, mischief always lurked around the corner. One time when my brothers and I rehearsed with Mom at the piano, to keep us from pestering each other, she put us in three different corners of the room while we practiced. As the youngest (my brothers were six and eight years older than I), "it" was never my fault. I never instigated mischief nor did I ever confess even if I had been the instigator. Maybe I should tell you that I was the more innocent brother, too.

My maternal grandparents were Lucien and Crystal Collins, and I have great childhood memories of spending time on their farm in Willow Branch, Indiana, about an hour east of Indianapolis. Whether Dad pastored in New Albany, Columbus, or Indianapolis, we had a relatively easy drive to visit them.

My brothers and my cousin Tom Collins and I spent hours building forts and tunnels in the hayloft of Grandpa's barn. We constructed intricate mazes in the upper level of this huge wooden structure. Although today that barn would seem small, it was a wonderland for young boys. Kids who grow up in an urban or even suburban setting have no concept of the simple pleasures of playing in such a fortress.

Grandpa grew a variety of crops including corn and soybeans. He also had pigs, chickens, and some dairy cows. I remember watching Grandpa in the milking room where the cows lined up. He would attach the automated milking machines to their udders and soon, I would see raw, unpasteurized milk being poured into milk cans, which would be picked up later and taken to be pasteurized, bottled, and sold. Grandpa took great pride in his farm and what he had accomplished. And, of course, there were a myriad of cats to keep mice from eating the grain. Farm life was hard, unrelenting work with daily chores that never ended.

One day, I accidentally unleashed a torrent of corn that Grandpa had stored in a room on the barn's ground floor. This was just a regular room filled with dried corn from floor to ceiling to feed the livestock. Grandpa had cut a rectangular hole in a door with a piece of burlap tacked across the top. He tucked the bottom of the burlap into the bottom of the hole and the weight of the corn against the burlap created a kind of dam to restrict the corn's flow. When Grandpa needed corn to feed the cows, he put a bucket under the hole and pulled the burlap to release the corn.

On that fateful day, I tugged at the burlap and the corn began to flow. It rained corn! Desperately, I tried to tuck the burlap back into place to stop it. Didn't happen. As a mountain of corn grew at my feet, I imagined Grandpa discovering the mess and punishing me. I was in a panic. How I wished that either Phil or Bill were nearby so that I could put the blame on one of them.

When Grandpa rounded the corner, my fear of his wrath was unfounded. He firmly tucked the burlap back into place and stopped the flow. Grandpa wasn't a man of many words, but a smile and a pat on the head let me know that all was well. He was a wonderful picture of grace to a fear-filled child.

Steve's parents, W.A. and Virginia Amerson, with Steve

STEVE AMERSON

Getting to the farm was sometimes an adventure in itself as we drove narrow two-lane roads through the fields of Indiana. On one occasion, I made the drive with my brothers in our family's Dodge Lancer. It was just the three of us. I was in the back seat while Phil and Bill, who were teenagers, sat in the front. Just because they could, they decided to change positions from the driver's seat to the passenger's seat while driving. Part of the joy was knowing that they were putting me into a state of absolute terror as they attempted that maneuver. "Guys, cut it out. You're gonna kill us," I hollered over and over. Obviously, we survived, but the event is seared into my brain. In retrospect, that experience served me well for navigating the Los Angeles freeways.

Looking back, I can see that my brothers had one basic goal: "Let's torment Steve." What they didn't know was that it worked in my favor and made me tough. When I was in elementary school, we lived in Indianapolis, and I started playing organized sports. I loved football and thought about becoming a professional football player. Eventually I realized I was too small and too slow.

At our home in Indianapolis, my brothers often made me run pass patterns in the backyard. They threw the football at me as hard as they could to see if I could catch it and if they could knock me down. Their intent was to do both. Unknowingly, they also made me resilient, which turned out to be a blessing.

Later, my dad pastored Dueber United Methodist Church in Canton, Ohio, home of the National Football Hall of Fame. This was an area in which high schools like McKinley and Massillon were football dynasties. Those practice sessions with my brothers helped me make the football team in both junior and senior high school. And those experiences also prepared me for my future. Being involved in the performing world requires handling rejection. Often, I have auditioned for a soloist spot or for a commercial only to find that the decision was not based on talent but some other factor, including a relationship another singer might have had with the producer. It's all part of the business. Although I've had a blessed life with many opportunities, there have been some disappointments. Success, however, is not whether you get knocked down but whether you get back up.

My grandparents were stalwarts in the tiny Willow Branch United Methodist Church, which had a sanctuary that sat 200 people at most. Grandpa was Sunday School Superintendent and Grandma Crystal was the organist. How I loved attending potluck dinners in the basement of the church. Memories of the homemade dishes from those rural chefs still make my mouth water. Julia Childs had nothing on those cooks. Boxed Pillsbury mixes? No way. This food was made-from-scratch delicacies. At the church dinners and at Thanksgiving dinners at my grandparent's home, I savored Grandma's creamed corn, homemade gravy, and her astounding yeast rolls. Indescribable. And the good news was that there was always plenty so I didn't need to worry about my brothers grabbing the last roll.

One Sunday evening my father preached at a revival service at Willow Branch United Methodist Church. My grandma was at the Hammond organ, providing accompaniment for the congregational singing. The wooden floors creaked as they exposed the years of worshipers walking down the aisles to the altar at the front of the platform. Countless tears were shed at that altar as country folk knelt on those benches and sought God for healing, broken relationships, and even for rain to refresh parched fields. It was a sacred place.

In those days, we sang from a hymnal—this was long before the use of video projection and screens found in most churches today. Sadly, the art of four-part congregational singing has almost disappeared, but back then it wasn't uncommon for a song leader to occasionally ask the instruments to stop playing so that the unaccompanied voices filled the sanctuary with harmony. If you grew up in that tradition, you might have memories of gospel songs like "Wonderful Grace of Jesus." On the chorus, the basses sang the melody while the upper three voices added a beautiful counter melody. As a youth, I wondered if it were okay to have this much fun singing as the different vocal parts blended.

On that revival night, I stood next to my mom. I was about four years old, and we were singing an old gospel song "My Sheep Know My Voice." As I sang out, I saw mom look down at me with a perplexed expression on her face.

"Uh oh," I thought. "I'm in trouble for something. She's gonna lead me out of this pew, take me to the women's bathroom, and give me a swat." I'm sure you wonder how such an angelic child as I could ever deserve any discipline. Normally, the swat wasn't an issue. It really didn't hurt, but it sure got my attention on the "rare" occasions when I misbehaved. Even at four years of age, however, the true punishment was the embarrassment of being hauled into the women's bathroom.

But Mom just stood there and looked at me. Her astonishment wasn't because I had been disobedient, but because at age four, I was singing a harmony part. I didn't know that was out of the ordinary. I was just singing like everyone else in the congregation.

That moment of harmony in a rural church was a precursor of things to come, an indicator that I had musical ability, which would lead me to sing in choirs, play the piano, accordion, and guitar, take voice lessons, and eventually earn bachelor's and master's degrees in music. On that night, I was only a small child in a small church in a small farming community in rural Indiana. Yet, God rejoiced in that moment as I began to let the talent that He had given me start to blossom and grow. It would be easy to dismiss that moment when a little boy sang a simple gospel song in a simple country church—but as I know now, God uses small beginnings.

ENCORE

Our words have power. Speak an encouraging word to a child today.

STEVE AMERSON

CHAPTER TWO

Making Harmony with Kristine

"Let your wife be a fountain of blessing for you.
Rejoice in the wife of your youth."

— Prov. 5:18

I spent my junior and senior high school years in Canton, Ohio, where teams played some pretty aggressive football. Thanks to my brothers, I learned to love feeling the crack of my shoulder pads against my opponents. There was something gratifying about giving a great block or making a devastating tackle that left the opposing player question whether he wanted to run in my direction again.

In addition to playing sports, I studied piano and yes, I admit it—I took accordion lessons. In high school, I also took private voice lessons, sang in the choir, and participated in most of the musical and theatrical opportunities at Lincoln High School. My credits included singing the role of Charlie Dalrymple in *Brigadoon* and Prince Dauntless in *Once upon a Mattress*. Although everything was building toward my future, I had no idea where these musical and theatrical endeavors would take me.

When I was thirteen, my brother Bill received a guitar for his birthday. Almost immediately, I picked up his guitar and taught myself to play. Bill was really miffed at my natural ability to learn some chords and make music. Impressed, my parents bought me my own KAY guitar. I continued to learn more chords and gain some proficiency. After proving my ability on that inexpensive six string, I stepped up to a Gibson guitar that cost about $250. I spent hours listening to the folk and pop artists of the day as I tried to figure out how they played the songs they played.

In those days, vinyl records were the delivery system. This was before CDs, cassettes, or even eight-track tapes. My search to understand the correct way to play certain songs and guitar licks required my lifting the needle from the record, placing it back on the disc, and listening again and again. It's a wonder that I never broke the arm or the needle on my stereo. My tutors were the great folk artists of the day: Peter, Paul, and Mary, Pete Seeger, James Taylor, and Joni Mitchell. Over and over, I was "Leaving on a Jet Plane" in the midst of "Fire and Rain." My brother, Bill would have been thrilled if I'd left on that airplane, but I know that he was actually proud that his little brother was coming into his own. Plus, I wasn't using his guitar any longer. Of course, neither was he.

As I continued to improve, I sold my Gibson guitar and bought my treasured Martin D-18. I still own that guitar, complete with the nicks and scratches of fifty years. With my precious Martin, I played for the Young Life club and church events as well as traveled and sang for youth events across northern Ohio. I also began writing songs based on what I had gleaned from those artists who had unknowingly been my mentors. By their example, they had taught me the basics of lyric writing and the fundamentals of song structure. That Martin guitar not only became a means to develop my musical ability, but also an instrument to connect with my future wife, Kristine. More about that later.

Through my sophomore year at Lincoln High School, I played football. One Friday afternoon at practice, I was knocked out by a devastating block from another player. As I regained consciousness, I could hear Coach Andretti yell, "Who's down out there? Get him off the field! Get him off the field!" At that moment, I had a revelation that music might be a safer career path than the NFL. I hung up my football cleats and ran cross-country for the next two years of high school to stay active and in shape. I wasn't particularly fast, but the chances of getting knocked unconscious were greatly reduced.

After graduating from Lincoln High School, I headed to Indiana for college. An audition at Bowling Green University earned me a full-ride music scholarship offer, but I decided on Taylor University, a small Christian liberal arts college in the cornfields of Northern Indiana. My dorm mates and I used to joke that Taylor was twenty miles from the nearest known sin.

Both of my brothers attended Asbury College in Wilmore, Kentucky, but I decided to strike out on my own. I had some familiarity with Taylor, which my mom attended for one year before leaving because of financial constraints. She completed her degree at Asbury College and met my father, who was attending Asbury Seminary.

Although Taylor University gave me some financial aid, it wasn't equal to the scholarship that Bowling Green University offered. Nevertheless, my parents sacrificed to provide for my education. Coming from meager, rural roots, both of them valued higher education. Thanks to a cousin's generosity, my father was able to attend seminary. When my turn came, Dad said, "Steve, we sent your brothers to Asbury, and we'll make Taylor work for you." Mom's income as a high school teacher in Canton helped cover the tuition costs for private colleges. Even today, I'm still grateful to my folks, who were "firmly planted by streams of water...[and] yielded fruit in its season" (adapted from Psa. 1:3).

I entered Taylor University as a voice major, but after that first semester, I went undeclared. I remained a music major but wasn't sure that focusing on singing was the right direction. As it turned out, I earned a bachelor of arts in music theory and composition. Years later, Taylor University awarded me an honorary doctorate. Being a music major at Taylor meant that I had to sing in several ensembles each semester. My freshman and sophomore years, I sang in the Oratorio Chorus, which was a large choir that performed major works like Handel's *Messiah*. Students with majors other than music often sang or played in an ensemble as a way to fulfill the elective class requirement. Many students thought that singing in an ensemble was an easy way to earn a credit. Chances of getting a passing grade were almost a sure thing and, of course, the risk of getting knocked unconscious from singing Handel was minimal.

Participation in the Oratorio Chorus came with a bonus: Kristine Hayes. I was a sophomore when I first saw the pretty, dark-haired freshman who sat in the alto section several rows behind me. Like many others, she was there to fulfill a required elective. Growing up in the church music world had been a part of her life, and she sang in a Youth for Christ ensemble while in high school.

I saw her in our weekly rehearsals. And in her Fine Arts class, she heard me sing "Greensleeves" while accompanying myself on the guitar. I learned that she had dated quite a few guys, but even so, she accepted my invite for a date. Maybe playing the guitar sealed the deal. On our dates, I often sat on the dorm steps and played. She heard the repertoire of songs I had taught myself from the records and some of the songs I had begun to compose. We dated steadily for a couple of years and then became serious in my junior year.

Since I was required to attend a certain number of concerts each semester, many of those concerts became opportunities to get to know the future Mrs. Steve Amerson. As we dated, we took in a variety of concerts including a performance of the twentieth-century atonal opera *Wozzeck* by Alan Berg, which was performed at Indiana University in Bloomington. If you don't know the opera, it's one of the more bizarre musical works out there. Maybe not romantic date, but I had a date with Kristine.

Whether a concert of bizarre music or a milkshake at Ivanhoe's Drive-In, Kristine was adventurous and always up for anything. A year after our wedding and on our move from Indiana to California, we happened upon a dirt road in the mountains of Arizona. The next thing I knew, she had convinced me to head up what barely passed for a road in my yellow, un-airconditioned Dodge Colt loaded with many of our earthly belongings, including my precious Martin guitar. What had she talked me in to?

Kristine loved bouncing from side to side over deep furrows that had been carved by recent rainstorms. Just when I thought it couldn't get any worse, I saw ominous rain clouds looming above us. Before the deluge started, I found a place to turn around and drove us out of there alive, without breaking an axle. Her adventurous streak continues to this day, and I've learned to give her room to do certain activities on her own. After all, someone needs to be around to spoil the grandchildren.

While we were college kids, we enjoyed other musical dates that weren't weird operas, like a concert with Christian artists Peter York and Phil Keaggy at neighboring Anderson University and a James Taylor concert at Blossom Music Center in Ohio. Music has a unique way of bringing people together, and we came to understand that "where words fail, music speaks."[1] During my senior year, I proposed and she said, "Yes." Great word: Yes!

After graduating from Taylor University, I headed to Southern Baptist Theological Seminary to pursue a master's degree in church music while Kristine finished her senior year. The music program at Southern was phenomenal and a degree from that institution practically guaranteed that I would find a job.

While still in seminary, I started singing on Monday nights in a Louisville bar called the Butchertown Pub. Those years of learning the songs of Peter, Paul and Mary, James Taylor, and other artists paid off. Each Monday night I walked out with forty dollars cash! Pretty good payday for 1976.

During that year we were apart, I made numerous long, red-eye drives from Louisville to Taylor University, and in the summer, I made the even longer drive to Trenton, Michigan, to spend time with Kristine. During the summer months, Kristine worked as a lifeguard and taught swimming at the local swimming pool, which also allowed her to work on her tan. Nice work if you can get it.

Many of my road trips followed my singing four fifty-minute sets at the pub, after which I jumped in the car to start the six-hour drive to Trenton. I thank God for my cassette player and my CB radio, which kept me from falling asleep. Often, I rolled the window down and stuck my head out to perk up. Using my CB handle of "Troubadour," I chatted with the truckers as I fought to stay awake. I never dozed off, and I never got a ticket as my 1973 Dodge Colt and I clipped along. On more than one occasion the words, "Ten-four, good buddy," crackled over my radio.

When we married on July 30, 1977, music was a major part of our wedding. Kristine had grown up at the First Baptist Church in Lincoln Park, Michigan, a suburb of Detroit. Her entire family was involved in the church. Her father, Ken Hayes, served on church boards and her mother, Evelyn, taught a Sunday School class for children with special needs. And to make sure that these children had rides to church, every Sunday, her dad drove a bus and picked them up. It was door-to-door dedication. That the church provided a special class and transportation was a testament to the church as well as to her parents.

Music for the wedding included the participation of Dr. Fred Shulze, who was my major professor. At Taylor, Fred taught piano, organ, and theory and composition courses. As a composition major, I spent countless hours with him while learning how to craft a melody and how to structure a song. Fred continued to build on the songwriting skills that I had developed with my Martin guitar.

As his student, Fred often asked me to stand at his side and turn pages as he played at organ recitals. The responsibility was intimidating as I wanted to make certain I didn't turn the page too early or too late. If I screwed up, a musical disaster and a groan from Fred would come my way. Fred not only played the organ for our wedding ceremony, but he also composed a processional march for the occasion. Since the pipe organ at the church was in need of repair and tuning, Kristine's father took on the additional expense to have that work done. He wanted everything to be perfect for his baby girl's wedding.

Music for the ceremony included the congregation singing of one of our favorite hymns: "Praise to the Lord, the Almighty." Fred also played several of the organ selections that I had heard when I turned pages for him in recitals. One of my favorite selections was "Prelude on Brother James Air" by M. Searle Wright. To this day I love the melody, harmony, and sonorities of this piece. My musical contribution to the ceremony was to sing the J. S. Bach setting of "O Love That Casts Out Fear" with Fred accompanying on the organ. Even though the ceremony itself was nerve-wracking, I was able to sing. Just to make sure I didn't forget the words, I typed them on a small piece of paper so I could hold them as I sang to Kristine. The lyric of the song was appropriate for the wedding, for the beginning of a marriage, and for our life together.

O love that casts out fear,
O love that casts out sin,
Oh, stay no more without
But come and dwell within.
True sunlight of the soul,
Surround us as we go;
So shall our way be safe,
Our feet no straying know.[2]

My father participated in officiating the service and near the close of the ceremony, both sets of parents came forward and prayed for us. Harmony between our families was beautiful from the beginning and continued through the years.

Kristine and Steve on their wedding day

Our wedding was the start of our shared musical experiences. The first year of our marriage, we lived in New Albany, Indiana, while I completed my degree in church music across the river at Southern Baptist Seminary in Louisville, Kentucky.

Southern Seminary provided a solid education in church administration and in leadership of musical programs while allowing me to continue my vocal studies.

During that year, Kristine did some substitute teaching, some waitressing, and some modeling across the river in Louisville, Kentucky. Always up for anything, she even modeled make-up used for corpses at a convention for morticians in Louisville. I had four part-time jobs while working on my master's degree and one of them was as a paid soloist at a church in Louisville. She joined the choir so that we could be together at rehearsals and services and also assisted me at one of my other jobs working with youth at a church in New Albany.

Another perk at Southern was the friendships that we developed. On one occasion, we organized a formal birthday party for a fellow student in the middle of a field complete with white linens, sterling silver, crystal, candles, and a piano in the back of a pickup truck. Life was a harmonious and sometimes hilarious whirlwind.

Once I finished seminary, we moved to California where I joined the staff of First Baptist Church of Van Nuys. The church had a phenomenal music program and while my initial job was to work with college and single adults, Kristine and I also sang in the choir.

Years later, I would become Minister of Music at the church, and Kristine would sing in the alto section while

I conducted the choir. One year, we sang in a group that provided music for corporate events and even sang for a special Fourth of July presentation at Disneyland. Since rehearsals within the Magic Kingdom had to take place in the middle of the night when no crowds were around, we didn't get much sleep. It was fascinating to see the park empty. Kristine also sang in the choral group on my recordings. On one project we sang a duet on the song "But As for Me and My House."

To this day, Kristine remains my best friend and biggest cheerleader, pulling for me whenever I'm on and off stage. She knows when I'm ill but still in the spotlight and singing through the sickness. Even from her seat in the audience, Kristine and I continue to harmonize. Over the years, we have come to believe that "next to the Word of God, the noble art of music is the greatest treasure in the world."[3]

ENCORE

There's no better way to grow close to others than to harmonize with them. If you feel alone, join a church or a community choir or a band. Nothing beats making music with others. You might even find a spouse.

CHAPTER THREE

Lessons from the Maestro

"In his grace, God has given us different gifts for doing certain things well. So if God has given you the ability to prophesy, speak out with as much faith as God has given you. If your gift is serving others, serve them well. If you are a teacher, teach well."

— Rom. 12:6–7

Kristine and I moved to California in 1978 and set off on our western adventure. Our thought was to return to our Midwestern roots after two or three years on the West Coast. We're still here.

When I began my work as Minister of College and Single Adults at the First Baptist Church of Van Nuys, Kristine and I became a part of the music program. The minister of music who oversaw this extensive music department was O. D. Hall. Even though I was head of a department on the church staff, O. D. welcomed Kristine and me to the adult Amen Choir. Even in churches you don't always find cooperation among different departments. That wasn't the case with O.

D. and me. He was thrilled to have Kristine join the altos and me join the tenors. O. D. and his wife, Elnora, were gracious to us and became close friends, a friendship that continues to this day.

The music program of the church was diverse. It encompassed classical sacred music and the best contemporary Christian music of the day. And the musicians in the choirs and ensembles included some of Los Angeles' finest session singers, music professors, and teachers. A dream team.

In 1979, O. D. was preparing the choirs for a presentation of Mendelssohn's *Elijah*. The performances would be fully staged and costumed, a huge undertaking that few churches would have attempted. To sing the role of Elijah, O. D. asked his long-time friend, David Ford, to join us. David had performed the role scores of times. Even in concert presentations in which the other soloists wore tuxedos or gowns, David performed in his own biblical robe and sandals. His appearance, along with his booming bass-baritone voice, was an impressive visual and aural experience.

O. D. asked me to sing the role of Obadiah, which allowed me to sing two of the most beloved sacred tenor solos: "If With All Your Hearts" and "Then Shall the Righteous Shine." What a joy to sing those oratorio arias with a full orchestra. Since this was a staged performance, there were scenes in which I would stand at David's side as he sang. I remember the first time that he cut loose singing right into my face. His voice just about blew me off the stage. I thought, "This is a Category Five hurricane force wind. Duck for cover!"

In my college and seminary days, I had some good teachers and some not-so-good teachers. Even at age twenty-four, my voice was still developing. It was like an

STEVE AMERSON

unruly stallion: lots of power and brilliant sound. But I didn't know how to rein it in nor did some of my teachers, who recognized the potential but didn't have the knowledge and techniques to train it.

During that production of *Elijah*, David asked who my voice teacher was. Although I had been searching for one, I hadn't yet found the right person in Los Angeles. Hearing the potential in my voice, David sensed my frustration. At one of the rehearsals, he said, "Steve, while I'm in Los Angeles, I'm going to drive to Montecito to visit Alan Rogers Lindquest. He's my former voice teacher. You know, Mr. Lindquest might be a great teacher for you, too. I'll ask him if he'll listen to you." True to his word, David Ford opened the door for me to study with Mr. Lindquest. A few weeks later, I headed north on the Ventura Freeway and drove ninety minutes to Montecito to meet the maestro. It was a drive that I would make hundreds of times in the coming years.

Mr. Lindquest was eighty-six years old. He walked with a cane and his stature had inevitably shrunk, but his spirit was strong and there was a twinkle in his eye. Over the next seven years, he became my mentor, my friend, and my guide.

He was born in Chicago in 1891 to Swedish immigrant parents. And during World War I, he established himself as Thomas Edison's favorite recording tenor. He was also a starring tenor on the vaudeville circuit and earning a minimum of $1,000 a week. In those days, that was huge money. His solo career flourished, and he was one of the two most famous tenors in New York at the time. In 1917, he sang for Enrico Caruso. Caruso wanted Mr. Lindquest to go to Italy to study, but he chose to stick with his lucrative career in the United States.

Mr. Lindquest's career mirrored mine. In New York City, he had sung vaudeville under the name Alan Rogers and classical music under the name, Alan Lindquest. Prejudice between the styles existed even then. I was a Los Angeles "session singer," performing for movies, commercials and television shows but also beginning my classical solo career. Mr. Lindquest understood that I had a foot in two different musical worlds.

Not only was Mr. Lindquest a phenomenal teacher, but he was also a man of faith. At the start of my lessons he would often say, "Pray that the Lord will ease your burden."

My years with him also taught me how to harness my spirit as well as my voice.

Steve with his teacher, Alan Rogers Lindquest

In the coming years, Mr. Lindquest became second set of ears for me. Even though he wore hearing aids, he was able to detect what was happening with my voice. We worked intently on a classical repertoire from oratorios and operas. His focus was on breathing and on vowel modification. In simple terms, vowel modification has to do with the way that a vowel changes based on the pitch being sung. Singing "day" at the bottom of my range would be sung differently than "day" at the higher end of my vocal range. The trick is to learn how to modify each vowel on each pitch. We spent hours on addressing how to approach a note based not only on the way that the vowel should sound but also on how it should feel.

He often had me lie on the floor while vocalizing or singing a passage. "Steve," he would say, "imagine the narrow of your back expanding and touching the floor as you inhale. This will help you understand that it's not how much air you take in when you inhale, but how efficiently you use that air as you sing!"

Describing the relationship and vulnerability that can exist between a voice student and the teacher is complicated. Not all relationships between teachers and students are productive. I have experienced that. I had a couple of teachers with whom there was no connection. It just didn't work. But when the student and teacher are on the same page vocally, emotionally, and spiritually, amazing things can happen. Mr. Lindquest and I had a phenomenal connection. Times that Kristine and I spent with Mr. and Mrs. Lindquest were glimpses into history. We were in our twenties, and these octogenarians shared the past and their wisdom with us. Hearing their stories of surviving the Great Depression gave us a new appreciation of our blessings.

Some musicians play an instrument—a piano, a violin, a trombone. When sick they might not give their best performance, but they can still deliver. For a singer, the body is their instrument. Swollen vocal chords can bring a singer to their knees and little can be done about it other than taking steroids to reduce inflammation of the vocal folds. While I've taken steroids a couple of times in emergency situations, I don't like doing it. Steroid medication might help me get through a performance, but it delays a full recovery.

During my training with Mr. Lindquest, he supported me in my classical and studio activities as well as in my church work. During those days, it was common for America singers to take a contract in European cities to learn languages and operatic roles. In 1983, Mr. Lindquest prepared me and encouraged both Kristine and me as we traveled to Germany and Switzerland where I auditioned in opera houses. The opera house in St. Galin, Switzerland, offered me a contract. Although accepting a contract in an overseas opera house would have changed the trajectory of our lives and of my career, Mr. Lindquest fully supported me when I decided to stay in the states to continue my music position at the church and to develop my budding classical concert career and studio work.

When I was in my late twenties, Mr. Lindquest told me what would happen with my voice in years to come. "Steve, when you're around thirty-three, your voice will become fuller and richer. And the size of your chest should increase, too. Right now, you're what, 38 or 39 inches? I want your chest to be around 44 inches because that will bring strength and grounding to your vocal production."

In February of 1984, Mr. Lindquest was scheduled for cataract surgery. Prior to the operation, the doctor took Mr. Lindquest off his regular medication, which caused him to experience congestive heart failure. His wife, Martha, called to tell me that he had been taken to Cottage Hospital in Santa Barbara. This was totally unexpected.

Kristine and I drove to Santa Barbara so that we could spend time with my mentor and my friend. When I entered the hospital room, he was very weak but he asked in a whisper, "How's the Japanese?" He and I had been working on arias from Puccini's Madam Butterfly. "Mr. Lindquest, my practice is going well. You'll be proud."

Then, in a labored voice he said, "You have brought me so much joy." That's when I lost it. I knew that my days with this gentle man, this beloved maestro, were coming to an end. With his hand in mine and with a barely audible tone, he struggled to say, "I shall see Him face to face."

With those words, a medical alert sounded and the nurse asked us to leave the room so that they could put him on a ventilator. When we returned to his side, he could no longer speak. With tears streaming down my face I said, "I love you." Sensing that he was hanging on for me, I whispered, "I will be okay." These words of assurance were my feeble attempt of letting him go.

The next morning, my mentor and guide stepped into eternity. As my own father used to say, "He caught a glimpse of heaven and it took his breath away." Mr. Lindquest slipped into the presence of God to "see Him face to face."

After Mr. Lindquest's passing, I attempted to find another voice teacher. It was fruitless until I finally connected with someone who had trained with William Vennard, another teacher influenced by Mr. Lindquest. Finding a kindred spirit who understood this philosophy of vocal production gave me hope.

When I turned thirty-three, my voice broadened and became fuller, just as Mr. Lindquest told me it would. I experienced months of frustration trying to figure out how to manage a voice that had become so rich and full. And yet through those challenging days, I remembered his teaching me to sing the way that it felt and not the way that it sounded. Mr. Lindquest didn't want me listening to myself, but trusting the way that he taught me to breathe and the way that each vowel should feel.

Even now, especially when I'm a bit under the weather, I concentrate on how my singing feels in my head and throat and not how it sounds. And in troubled times just as Mr. Lindquest suggested, I continue to ask the Lord to ease my burden. Oh, and just in case you were wondering, my jacket size is a 44 regular.

ENCORE

Our elders have much to teach us. Spend some time with someone who can share their wisdom and experience with you.

Chapter Four

Under the Stars
at the Hollywood Bowl

"For God has not given us a spirit of fear and
timidity, but of power, love, and self-discipline."

— 2 Tim. 1:7

One of the joys of living near Los Angeles is attending
concerts at the Hollywood Bowl. It doesn't matter if
the concert features the Los Angeles Philharmonic, a night
of jazz, or a *Sound of Music* sing-a-long, there's something
special about that setting nestled in a valley just north of
Hollywood Boulevard. This 18,000-seat venue sits in the
middle of an urban jungle, a cultural oasis where treasured
concert experiences reside adjacent to the hectic Hollywood Freeway. Apart from the occasional airplane or helicopter that flies overhead, a night at the Bowl is like being in
a remote forest surrounded by tall trees and wildlife.

Sitting in the bleacher seats is enjoyable, but oh the
delight of having box seats in which you can feast on a
scrumptious meal and then sip a nice glass of wine as the
music fills the atmosphere on a summer evening. Sharing

a night at the Hollywood Bowl with friends is a recipe for lasting memories.

I had experienced some success as a soloist with the Los Angeles Master Chorale under the direction of Roger Wagner, which gave me credibility in the Los Angeles classical music community. Even so, every Sunday, I continued to scour the *Los Angeles Times Calendar* section for the letters "TBA" whenever the newspaper listed the soloists for an upcoming concert. That was my clue that the soloists had not yet been hired.

While in high school in the 1970s, I grew a mustache. It was a trendy thing to do, and I kept the mustache and sometimes even sported a full beard through my college and master's degree days. What can I say? It was the 1970s.

Shortly after arriving in Los Angeles, I was asked to sing the role of Obadiah in a staged version of Mendelsohn's *Elijah*. For the role, I grew a full beard, which was appropriate for the presentation, but also made me look older. I was in my mid-twenties and my full, dynamic tenor voice belied my youth. I thought keeping the beard would give me credibility as I auditioned for classical music jobs. It worked. With that full beard and a clarion tenor voice, I landed an engagement to be a soloist in the presentation of Igor Stravinsky's *Canticum Sacrum* (Sacred Song) at the Hollywood Bowl.

For a young, developing solo artist, singing at a venue as iconic as the Hollywood Bowl was a dream. But to be a soloist with the Los Angeles Philharmonic under the baton of Maestro Michael Tilson Thomas on that stage was the promised land. After living in LA for a few years, I understood the significance of being a featured soloist at the Hollywood Bowl.

Canticum Sacrum was a new work to me and not a part of the standard literature such as the *Messiah* or other oratorio and concert works. If you do a Wikipedia search, you will learn the following:

> *Canticum Sacrum ad Honorem Sancti Marci Nominis* is a 17-minute choral-orchestral piece composed in 1955 by Igor Stravinsky (1882–1971) in tribute "To the City of Venice, in praise of its Patron Saint, the Blessed Mark, Apostle." The piece is compact and stylistically varied, ranging from established neoclassical modes to experimental new techniques. The second movement, "Surge, Aquilo" represents Stravinsky's first movement based entirely on a tone row.[4]

Did you get all that? Wikipedia's complex explanation simply means that this piece by Stravinsky is hard as nails! Throughout the years, I have had to learn many difficult pieces of music. This was one of the toughest. The meter or time signature constantly changed, sometimes every bar. And the time signatures were not the typical 3/4 and 4/4. They were 4/8 to 5/16 to 7/16 to 8/16 to 7/16 to 3/8 and on and on. Even if you're not a musician, you might understand the overwhelming rhythmic complexity of the music. Obviously, I didn't have enough fingers to keep count. *Canticum Sacrum* was a Stravinsky mind game.

As for the melody of this composition: well, there is no melody at least not in the traditional sense. To the average person, the melody sounds as if someone tossed a bunch of magnetic musical notes against a steel wall with a musical staff painted on it and said, "That'll do." Based on a "tone row," the leaps and intervals required hours of pounding out pitches on the piano over and over until they were embedded in my ear and brain.

Performing this piece wasn't just about having a nice voice. In fact, it didn't require a beautiful voice at all. It required intense concentration and musicianship. I didn't fully understand what I was committing to when I accepted the engagement, but I was smart enough to know that I would be in rarified air when I performed the work on that stage with that orchestra and that conductor. Maybe some of the lessons that Phil and Bill instilled in me helped me focus on the task that lay ahead. Be tough. Press on.

I first met Maestro Tilson Thomas at a rehearsal at a secluded house on the property of the Hollywood Bowl. Trying to locate this property up the hill and behind the Bowl without a modern GPS was a navigational challenge. I struggled through the winding road as I tried to follow the directions that I'd been given. When I finally found the house, I knocked lightly on the door and hoped that I was at the correct location. I don't remember much about the rehearsal, but I could tell that Maestro Tilson Thomas was pleased with what I brought to the work. He realized that I had done intense homework on a treacherous piece of music, and his demeanor was reassuring.

What I clearly recall, however, is that in all of our rehearsals, as well as in the performance, Michael gave me every meticulous musical cue. Although I had the piece memorized, I constantly referred to the score just to make sure I didn't trip up. Tilson Thomas guided me through the demanding work as if he were holding my hand through the constant maze of meter changes. He provided a calm and gracious invitation for each vocal entrance of each phrase because he knew that one errant step would make my getting back on course virtually impossible. Only an instrumentalist or a singer can fully appreciate this level of comfort when facing a daunting work. I am forever grateful for Tilson Thomas' masterful direction. He did what few conductors could have done.

At the performance, I sat in the middle of the orchestra. Surrounded on three sides by some of the finest musicians in the world, I looked out on the 18,000 seats in front of me. My wife, Kristine, had the joy of sitting in a box with friends while I sweated it out on stage. I wasn't actually sweating, but it was intense work. Under the evening sky on this July night, the air was cool. Kristine was wrapped cozily in a shawl while I sat onstage in my recently purchased white dinner jacket. She had listened to hours of my sitting at the piano implanting the notes into my head, but even she couldn't comprehend the challenge before me.

As I looked over the audience, I had the presence of mind to tell myself: "Steve, remember this moment." Even at age twenty-five, I knew this was an unforgettable night. I also dreamed of a time when I could afford a stereo system that would approximate the luscious sonorities, harmonies, and textures I experienced while sitting in the middle of that world-class orchestra. "Remember this feeling. Remember this sound. Remember this night."

As I stood to sing my solo movement titled "Surge Aquilo," the adrenaline dropped into my stomach and began to burn.

I felt utter panic. "What in the heck have I gotten myself into? Get a grip."

For the first few seconds, I sang in sheer terror, but then reminded myself of the words I had written on the inside front cover of my score: "God hath not given [me] a spirit of fear, but of power, and of love, and of a sound mind" (2 Tim. 1:7).

The good news: I negotiated the difficult work successfully and received a rousing ovation from the crowd and the orchestra, which is normally a tougher critic than those who pay to attend. The audience for a concert of Igor Stravinsky music knew what to expect, and we had not disappointed them.

A couple of months later, I saw Maestro Tilson Thomas at the Hollywood Bowl where he was again conducting. Although I was in the audience for this concert, I negotiated myself backstage where Michael signed a picture of the two of us that had been taken at the prior concert.

His inscription read, "To Stephen, with infinite bravissimo for a superb "Surge Aquilo." Sempre avanti and love. Michael Tilson Thomas."

Years later, the memory of singing that "sacred song" remains fresh. And it continues to remind me of the Apostle Paul's words to Timothy: "God has not given us a spirit of fear; but of power and love and of a sound mind" (2 Tim. 1:7).

Steve with Maestro Michael Tilson Thomas at the Hollywood Bowl.
Photo by Larry Sterling

ENCORE

My dad used to say, "Fear is the darkroom where negatives are developed." Although in this digital age, his words may not have quite the same impact, consider one step you can take to overcome your fears today.

CHAPTER FIVE

Just as I Am

"As iron sharpens iron, so a friend sharpens a
friend."

— Prov. 27:17

One door can open another—or not. Over the years I
have been asked to sing at different events for the
exposure. A host will contact me and ask me to give of my
time and talent for a particular event or cause. Oftentimes,
the pitch will be "This could be good exposure for you." Oh
yeah! But I've learned that I can't pay my phone bill with
exposure. Singing is not a hobby. Singing is my job. It's my
calling. It's the way I make my living and the way I support my
family. But there have been those rare occasions in which I
sang for "exposure," and occasionally they turned out well.

In 1986, I signed a recording contract with Light Records.
A record deal is the dream of most singers because it means
you've finally arrived. Later on, I learned that a record deal
is not all that it's cracked up to be. In a contract, things like
"cross-collateralization" can see to it that artists never earn
any money from their recordings. It's all in the fine print.

Legendary musician Ralph Carmichael founded Light Records and Lexicon Music. Ralph was a respected name in the music business having arranged for artists including Nat King Cole, Bing Crosby, Ella Fitzgerald, and a host of others. Ralph was also a pioneer in Christian music with the youth musical, *Tell It Like It Is,* and numerous other compositions. The song, "Pass It On," came from that musical and was a huge hit in both Christian and secular markets. In the late 1960s, Ralph's use of guitars and drums in church music was revolutionary and even considered heresy in some churches. And yet, this use of "modern" musical idioms continues to reach scores of young people.

So I signed a one-record deal with Light Records. The project, *Shine On Me*, was released on vinyl and cassettes. Remember cassettes? At least the project wasn't released on eight-track. Paul Stilwell, who became a good friend, produced the recording. Paul had hired me for my first Los Angeles session work—singing demos for Lexicon Music. The budget for my record project was $10,000 and used five accompaniment tracks from the company's library as well as included the creation of five new selections. I had a real photo shoot with a professional photographer and worked with the graphic designer on the layout of the artwork for the cassette and album jacket. It was a humble start, but it was a start. While sales of this project were modest, it validated that I was a serious artist in the marketplace. The album also gave me a product to sell when I began touring as well as provided a repertoire and tracks for me to sing in concert. It was a step in the right direction.

About a year later, Ralph asked me to sing at the Western National Religious Broadcasters breakfast at a Los Angeles downtown hotel. I would be singing a couple of the songs from that first project, *Shine On Me*. While this convention was primarily for Christian broadcasters from western states, folks from all across the country would be in attendance. Although performing for the breakfast was an opportunity for exposure, it required me to sing at 7:00 a.m. Singing that early is a challenge for any artist. Over the years, however, I've been able to make it happen. When I started touring, I learned what it took to sing at an 8:00 a.m. worship service on the East Coast, which translated to 5:00 a.m. on the West Coast. I trained my body to "ignore the clock, shut up, and deliver!" Several months later, I found out that singing for that early morning breakfast had opened another door. Exposure.

In the summer of 1988, Kristine and I had dinner with Rig and Julie Dees, whom we knew from church. Most folks have heard of radio and television personality Rick Dees, whose given name is Rigdon. On that particular evening Rig challenged me. "Steve," he said, "I don't think you're doing what you're supposed to be doing. Look, I know you're a good at what you do and that the church loves you. But you're not fully using the gift of your singing voice." Rig was my wake-up call.

Over the next few weeks, I began to consider Rig's challenge. And in late August, I resigned my position at the First Baptist Church of Van Nuys, a decision made in consultation with some good friends and with significant times of prayer. My plan was to establish Amerson Music Ministries and to begin traveling and singing.

In my final weeks on the staff of the church, I received a phone call from Cliff Barrows. Now, anyone who had grown up in the church knew the name Cliff Barrows. Cliff was the music and program director for the Billy Graham Evangelistic Association. He was calling to see if I would be interested in singing at a Billy Graham Crusade in Hamilton, Ontario, Canada. You bet I would!

Even when I arrived in Hamilton, I had no idea how the invitation to sing for the crusade had come about. But it coincided with my decision to leave my job at the church and strike out on my own. I felt that it was confirmation of my choice to take a risk and trust God to provide. In Hamilton, I got to know Bob Straton, who worked for the Walter Bennett Company, the organization that booked the televised Billy Graham crusades on broadcast outlets. Bob was also a fellow singer who appreciated my voice. He searched me out and introduced himself. As we chatted, I told him that I didn't know how I wound up on Cliff's radar. "I can tell you how," Bob said. "I heard you sing at the Los Angeles breakfast and was impressed. So I recommended you to Cliff." Singing at that 7:00 a.m. breakfast paid off. Exposure.

On the day of the crusade, a singer's worst nightmare struck. I was sick. My swollen vocal cords made it tough to talk, let alone sing. On top of that, I was thousands of miles from my trusted ear nose and throat specialist, Dr. Hans von Leden, the voice doctor to celebrities and singers like James Taylor and opera star, Carol Neblett. If I could only see Dr. von Leden, maybe he could help. Not an option.

The morning of the crusade Cliff Barrow's secretary, Belma Ruth, called. "Steve, there will be a meeting in in Mr. Barrow's room at 10:00 a.m." Exactly at 10:00 a.m., I knocked on Cliff's door. Cliff warmly greeted me, invited me in, and offered me a Dr. Pepper before we began to talk. I was so nervous. Here I was, occupying the time of this revered man of God while waiting for the others to arrive so that the meeting could start. Then it struck me. The meeting was just with me. Cliff Barrows wanted to get to know me. *How is it that Cliff just wants to spend time with me?* I wondered.

To put things in context, in my family, Cliff Barrows, George Beverly Shea, and Billy Graham were akin to the Trinity. These men were spiritual giants and being in their presence was almost holy. A bit extreme? Well, maybe, but my family and I held these men in that high regard.

As Cliff and I talked, I tried not to let on that I wasn't feeling my best. I was taking every remedy I could think of, drinking lots of water, and praying that I could deliver that evening.

Later in the day, a driver loaded Kristine and me into a van and drove us from the hotel to the arena in which the crusade would be held. The driver took us into the bowels of the venue in the secure backstage area where a worker then escorted me to the stage to do a sound check on the two selections I would sing. My first number was "We the Redeemed" a song written by Howard McCrary, a friend from the Light Records project. This song had a pre-recorded track. I also selected an old gospel song, "My Heavenly Father Watches Over Me," with Ted Smith at the piano and John Innes at the organ, both of whom were extraordinary musicians. I did the best I could with the limited voice that I had as the engineers dialed in the levels for the sound in the arena and for the telecast. Following my sound check, I went backstage where Kristine and I shook hands with Bev Shea and Billy Graham, both of whom were so gracious in welcoming us. We had met all three members of the trinity!

Kristine's parents traveled to Hamilton from Michigan and my parents traveled from Canton, Ohio. They told everyone they encountered that their son and son-in-law was the one singing on the platform. Parental pride reached a new level that night.

Kristine and I were seated onstage among other platform participants and pastors who were part of the local committee that had organized the crusade. As the service began, I was surrounded by tens of thousands of people including hundreds that were part of the choir in the rows behind me. Here I was, seated on one of the most significant religious platforms in the world, surrounded by giants of the Christian faith, and participating in an evening with Billy Graham. I took a mental picture of that astounding opportunity—a genuine Kodak moment.

Soon Cliff Barrows was at the podium giving my introduction. I stood and did my best even though my voice was not all that I wanted it to be. One friend who watched the telecast said that I didn't sound sick, but he could see in my eyes that I wasn't feeling great. Following my two selections, I made my way back to my seat, thankful that I had completed the task. What and honor! What an opportunity. What exposure!

Then, Dr. Graham moved to the podium to give his simple, clear message of salvation in that North Carolina accent for which he was known. As the service drew to a close, he extended the invitation for people to come forward. While I stood on the platform singing "Just As I Am" with the crowd and the choir, a flood of people poured down the stairs and through the aisles all across the arena. They filled the entire space in front of the platform.

Back in my college days, my friends and I often jokingly repeated Dr. Graham's words as he extended the invitation: "If you came in a bus, the bus will wait." We weren't malicious, just kids uttering a familiar line as we waited for a buddy to join us. But when I stood on the platform and heard Dr. Graham speak those words himself, I was humbled and moved to tears. I also had the honor of singing in crusades in Albany, New York, in 1990 and at the Meadowlands in New Jersey in 1991.

A few months after that first crusade in Hamilton, Cliff and Bev were scheduled to do an event in Lancaster, Pennsylvania, for radio station WDAC, a station that played my music. Cliff was going to speak and, of course, Bev would sing. But when Bev became sick with bronchitis, Cliff called to see if I might be available to fill in. Think of it. I was going to fill in for George Beverly Shea! I wondered if the crowd of about 1,500 would revolt when they heard that Bev wasn't there and that this kid was his stand-in.

It turned out to be a great night and once again, being with Cliff was a joy. I sang "My Heavenly Father Watches over Me," which I had sung at the earlier crusade. When the evening ended, Cliff said to me, "You sang that differently than you did in Hamilton."

"You're right. I did. Tonight I had my voice."

I worked with Cliff several other times up until his death including events at the Billy Graham Training Center known as The Cove. At one particular event, I was on the platform singing when I noticed Dr. Graham quietly enter the auditorium. This was unusual because he was suffering from Parkinson's disease and getting around was difficult for him. To see this man of God slip into the room as I was singing was another memorable moment.

On one occasion Cliff and I did an event in Atlanta with a 300-voice choir. As Cliff led the audience in "How Great Thou Art," I was on the platform about six feet behind him. By this time he had almost lost his eyesight. But as he led the group, he turned back toward me and said, "Steve, is that you I hear? Come and sing the next verse." Even now, it humbles me whenever I remember his generous spirit.

Steve with Cliff Barrows

STEVE AMERSON

Cliff Barrows, this great servant of God, was a huge influence in my life. He became my friend because he loved and accepted me just as I am.

ENCORE

I never could have imaged winding up on the platform with Billy Graham, Cliff Barrows, and Bev Shea. Dream big. If you think too small, you might get in God's way.

CHAPTER SIX

Gifts from God

"Children are a gift from the LORD; they are a
reward from him."

— Ps. 127:3

My dad used to say, "We have six grandchildren and two
of them are adopted. I just can't remember which two."
That was my dad.

Kristine and I always anticipated that we would have
children, but we weren't in a hurry about it. We figured it
would happen in God's time. But after seven or eight years of
marriage, medical consultations, and God's time not having
come, we began to explore adoption. One evening, we had
dinner with Byron and Kim Hornaday, friends from church.

"We've missed seeing you guys," I said.

"We haven't been at church for several weeks," Kim
said. "We just adopted a baby, and we're staying home until
we get a routine worked out." As we had dinner, their story
unfolded. They had no idea that we had been considering
adoption. That "chance" dinner led to further conversa-
tions and eventually to an attorney who assisted us in the

adoption process. In less than a year, our son, Matthew, was part of our family.

During these days, Kristine worked as a real estate appraiser, and I was Minister of Music at First Baptist Church of Van Nuys. My responsibilities at the church were significant as I oversaw a vibrant music program with a 110-voice adult choir, a college/career choir, a high school choir, junior high choir, six children's choirs, hand bells and vocal and instrumental ensembles. Even though I had a staff to assist me, I was a busy public figure in the church and in the community as well.

When people find out that a couple is going to adopt, it's common for them to say, "Oh, now you're going to get pregnant." Although they're well meaning, that actually happens less than 10 percent of the time. It's also not unheard of for disappointments to occur in the adoption process. If something goes awry, explanations of what happened or what didn't happen can be awkward and painful—much easier and safer to keep quiet until the adoption is a "done deal."

Around this time, I recorded a commercial for Delta Airlines in which I sang "Nessun dorma" from the opera *Turandot*. Originally, Delta wanted Luciano Pavarotti, but his fee to record the spot was in the millions. I wound up doing the commercial, and although I didn't earn the millions Pavarotti would have, it was still a pretty good payday. And a necessary one, too. Private adoption could be expensive as it was customary for the adoptive parents to cover the cost of the birth and other expenses incurred by the birthmother. Little did we know that the residuals from the Delta spot would help underwrite Matthew's adoption.

In December of 1986, Kristine and I had a meeting with a potential birthmother in an attorney's office in downtown, Los Angeles. The timing could not have been more challenging. It was the final week of rehearsals for *The Living Christmas Tree*, a huge presentation known by churches nationwide.

Each performance was an all-out production with 160 singers, dancers, a full orchestra, and an elaborate set. There would be sixteen performances over two weeks. The rehearsals and the performances were exhausting for the 400 dedicated volunteers who made the program happen.

In the final week of rehearsals for the production, Kristine and I spent an emotional day with the birthmother of our potential child. And on top of the pressures of preparing for the "Tree" and meeting a birthmother, I was sick. No voice whatsoever. Besides conducting the presentation, I was also expected to sing what had become a major dramatic solo at the end of each performance. *What next, Lord?* I wondered.

What next? Well, from that meeting, it appeared that a baby would be joining our family, and it would happen soon. Kristine and I decided to share the news with our close friends, Rick and Vicki Horne. We didn't tell anyone else. Rick was president of the church's adult choir, and Kristine and Vicki had started a gift business together. They were dear friends, and we trusted them to keep our potential adoption confidential.

On Friday morning, January 2, 1987, our baby was born a month earlier than expected in a Las Vegas hospital. Kristine was out when I received the call. Since this was before cell phones, I had no way of reaching her immediately. Eventually, Kristine arrived home, and I was waiting for her in the driveway. "Come on," I said. "Our baby's been born, and we need to get to Las Vegas as soon as possible."

We packed our bags and headed to the airport without a clue as to how long we would be gone. I called my assistant and said, "David, you're on standby to lead Sunday's worship." No explanation other than that. I also called Rick Horne and told him that Kristine and I were jumping on a flight to Las Vegas.

Think about it. It was New Year's weekend and the hotels and casinos were jammed with people in search of treasure. So were we, only our treasure would become a forever part of our family.

After landing in Las Vegas, Kristine and I took a taxi directly to the hospital to meet Matthew Wesley Amerson for the first time. The nurses checked our IDs to confirm that we were who we said we were. Then we put on hospital gowns and embraced the five-pound-fourteen-ounce baby boy. I found a payphone and called our friends, Rick and Vicki. "Rick, we just met our son. He's a healthy, beautiful boy."

"Well, of course he is. And Vicki and I are on our way to Las Vegas to meet the newest member of the Amerson family." These two people were the epitome of friendship: support and encouragement at just the right time. They didn't want us to be alone on this adventure.

Finding hotel rooms in Las Vegas on New Year's weekend was a challenge, but I managed to locate two rooms at a seedy hotel. After introducing the Hornes to Matthew at the hospital, we four adults went to a buffet at the Stardust Hotel and had a prime rib dinner for $4.95 each. Remember, this was the 1980s.

On Saturday morning, we went back to the hospital and were surprised to learn that the physician was ready to release Matthew to our care. Several hours later, we headed to the Las Vegas airport with our treasure. Returning home this time would be unlike any trip we had experienced before.

In 1987, airports were unrestricted—no TSA. You could walk around freely and see someone off or greet someone at the gate. Vicki, Rick, Kristine and I, with Matthew in tow, hurried to catch a flight from Las Vegas back to Los Angeles. The flight, however, was full, oversold actually, but we got on a standby list. In an act of desperation, I approached the gate agent and pointed at Kristine holding Matthew.

"Ma'am," I said, "that's my wife over there holding our son who was born yesterday. We're trying to get home. I know the flight is oversold, but if there is anything you could do, we would be grateful."

Within minutes the gate agent walked over to us with four boarding passes. That holiday season, there was room at the inn—I mean on the plane. Divine intervention.

During the brief flight to Los Angeles the woman sitting next to me started asking questions. "How old is your baby?"

"He was born yesterday."

She paused and then asked, "Where are you from?"

"We're from Los Angeles."

"Well, then where was he born?"

"Oh, he was born in Las Vegas."

"Did you plan on him being born in Las Vegas?" she asked, puzzled.

"Yes," I said, with a deadpan expression.

There was a long pause, and she took another look at Kristine holding Matthew. She practically shouted, "You look great!" I never told her that Matthew was our adopted baby. She's probably still trying to figure out how Kristine could have looked so great one day after Matthew's birth.

The next day, I stood on the platform at church, led worship and sang a solo. Before turning the service over to Dr. Jess Moody, the senior pastor, I said, "Kristine and I met a young man yesterday, and meeting him has changed our lives. Jess, I'd like for you and the congregation to meet him, too." Carrying our two-day old Matthew, Kristine walked onto the stage. The room exploded with joy and applause. Completely caught off-guard, Jess asked, "Is this yours?"

"Yes, Jess. He is ours."

A year later, I left my church position to begin a begin a concert ministry and to continue doing recording sessions in the Los Angeles studios. When I traveled and concertized, I often sang "Pray for The Children," a song I co-wrote. As a set-up for the number, I told about Matthew's adoption, including the story of the woman on the plane and her amazement at how amazing Kristine looked only one day after his birth. Audiences loved that story.

In the fall of 1991, a few weeks after a church concert, I received a call from a pastor of the church where I had sung. He shared that a young woman in his congregation was pregnant, and he wondered if Kristine and I had ever thought about adopting again. Little did he know that five-year-old Matthew had been praying each night for a sibling and that Kristine and I had quietly been considering a second adoption. Could this baby be the answer to Matthew's prayers?

On the Sunday before Thanksgiving, I did a concert back in Canton, Ohio. Remember Canton? That's the city where I spent my junior high and senior high school years. Kristine used my pager to request that I call home. She shared the news that Katherine had been born in Modesto, California. Packed and ready, Kristine was headed to Modesto with a friend to meet our daughter, Katherine. But I was in Canton and on my way to Nashville for a Thanksgiving Eve concert with Ronn Huff and a fifty-piece orchestra made up of the finest musicians in town. That stretch of time felt endless. But Baby Katherine didn't leave the hospital immediately. She had an infection and stayed for ten days to make sure that all would be well.

Even so, I was still stuck miles from Kristine, Matthew, and our new daughter. That's when Deaver and Chaz Corzine stepped up and invited me to their home for dinner and an impromptu baby shower with some of their friends. People with giving hearts are such blessings. As the old Latin phrase says, "A friend in need is a friend indeed."

The concert with Ronn Huff was magnificent—a packed house, but all I could think of was going home to California. On Thanksgiving morning, I jumped on the earliest flight to Los Angeles. After the plane landed, I rushed home to pick up Matthew, who was staying with friends. Then, the two of us flew to Modesto to see the baby that Matthew had prayed for. I think Matthew was probably hoping for a brother so his prayer should have been more specific. But as it turned out, Matt and Kat became a duo who continue to bless to us.

Kristine homeschooled Matt and Kat, which gave us great flexibility because they could study on the road as well as at home. When I traveled to sing for various events, the three of them would sometimes accompany me. Over the years, our family visited Alaska, New England, Canada, and the Bahamas, cruised through the Panama Canal, and even traveled to Israel.

Matt and Kat were a part of a homeschool group of about 250 families, which provided lots of activities: sports, music, and academic opportunities. Each year, the group held an elaborate graduation ceremony for all of its students to acknowledge each one, from a kindergartner to a gradu-ating senior. I was asked to sing at countless of these grad-uation ceremonies.

When Kat graduated from kindergarten, I sang the song "Lasso the Moon" while she sat on my lap. My close friend Lowell Alexander co-wrote the song. It was a touching moment made all the more touching twelve years later when Kat sat next to me in her high school cap and gown while I sang that same song with a video of her kindergarten graduation playing on a screen behind us. To view the video of "Lasso the Moon," go to www.steveamerson.com/lasso.

Steve with Katherine (Kat) at her high school graduation

Singing at graduations became part of my calling. In 2009, Mathew was a young man completing Basic Training at Fort Knox, Kentucky. Word got out that Matthew's dad was a singer who had sung at lots of events, including events honoring Medal of Honor recipients. So the commanding officer asked me to sing as Matthew and the other recruits completed their training. While Matthew stood proudly in his United States Army uniform, I opened the graduation ceremony with "The Star-Spangled Banner." Kristine, Kat, and other family members attended Matt's graduation. I was thrilled that my dad, who still couldn't remember which two of his grandkids were adopted, was also with us. And it was so fitting that Rick Horne, who had held that newborn baby twenty-two years earlier, was there to embrace Matthew once again.

Grandpa Amerson with Matthew and Steve
at Matthew's graduation from Boot Camp

Several years ago, Kristine and I were on a trip to Colorado. While browsing through an antique store, we discovered three worn lassos. We had each of them framed in a shadow box with the lyric of "Lasso the Moon" in the center. One hangs over the fireplace in our home and Matt and Kat each have one. And yes, I would lasso the moon for Kristine and our kids.

ENCORE

God always answers prayers. It might not be on our time schedule or in a way that we want. Don't miss the miracle that God wants to bring into your life, even if it comes in an unexpected way. He knows best.

CHAPTER SEVEN

If You're Going to Choke, Choke Together

"My heart, O God, is steadfast, my heart is
steadfast; I will sing and make music."

—Ps. 57:7

During my career, I've worked some wonderful conductors—names you might know like Christopher
Hogwood, Murray Sidlin, and Michael Tilson Thomas. I've
also worked with some lesser-known conductors who are
equally talented: Hector Guzman, Steven Byess, and Richard
Kaufmann. All of these conductors have a special place in
my memory.

One of the names most associated with choral music,
however, is Roger Wagner. Roger was an amazing man.
He was born in Le Puy, France, where his father was the
organist at the cathedral in Dijon. When Roger was twelve,
the family moved to United States, and at that young age,
Roger served as the organist at St. Ambrose Church in West
Hollywood. In 1931, Roger returned to France not only to
complete his musical studies, but also to serve in the French

army. In 1936, he qualified for the French decathlon team for the Summer Olympics. He returned to Los Angeles in 1937 and continued his music career. After the completion of the Los Angeles Music Center in 1964, he helped form the LA Master Chorale and directed that group for twenty years.

When I started my solo career in Los Angeles, Roger was the conductor of the chorale, which was one of the most respected choral groups in the nation, if not the world. Roger's crusty, cantankerous, demanding personality had something to do with that. He demanded excellence and could strike fear with his salty language and demeanor. During my time singing for him, I experienced his words of praise along with his wrath.

In the early 1980s, I decided to see if I could audition to do solo work for Roger and the Los Angeles Master Chorale. I called the Master Chorale office and inquired about auditioning for Roger. "The only way to get to Mr. Wagner is to audition for the chorale," said the receptionist. Singing in the chorale was demanding as they presented their own concerts as well as provided the chorus for Los Angeles Opera and Hollywood Bowl concerts. I had no time for singing in the chorale, but if auditioning for the chorale was the only way to get to Roger, so be it.

I scheduled an audition only to learn that Roger wouldn't even be in attendance. The first audition was held with an assistant who checked my vocal range and quality and sight-reading capabilities. It also entailed answering a list of ten musical term definitions. I knew the answer to nine of them, terms like *pianissimo* and *accelerando*, but I didn't know the term *assoluto*. Later, I learned that it meant absolute in Italian.

Now remember, I was young, somewhat irreverent and peeved at having to do the first audition without Roger even being there. So for the definition of assoluto I wrote: "A lute you play with your butt." Did I care what someone might think? No. Do I care now? No. I may be older but I'm still a bit of a rascal.

Assoluto notwithstanding, I made it through the first audition. A week or two later I returned to a room on the UCLA campus for my audition with Roger. He was seated at a table, head down, with his pipe drooping from his mouth. Plunging in, I said, "My name is Steve Amerson, and I'm especially interested in doing solo work for you."

"How original," he replied sarcastically. I can laugh about it now. Then—not so funny. "So, what are you going to sing for me?"

"I will be singing 'Il mio tesoro' from *The Magic Flute*." With that, the accompanist began the introduction while Roger stared at the tabletop as though he was more interested in refinishing it than he was in me.

When I began to sing, his eyes peered over his glasses, and he started to look at me. The more I sang, the more engaged he became. After I finished, he growled, "I want you in my chorale."

"I'm sorry, sir, but I don't have the time."

"I want you in my chorale, and I'll give your first shot at solo work."

"Thank you, but my schedule won't allow it." When I left the room, I figured that I would never hear from Roger Wagner again.

Two weeks later, I received a phone call from Robert Willoughby Jones, Executive Director of the Master Chorale.

He told me that the Master Chorale would be presenting two nights of two Gilbert and Sullivan works, *Trial by Jury* and *H.M.S. Pinafore*, and that they wanted me to sing the tenor leads in each work, which would be partially staged and in costume.

This would be my first professional classical job in Los Angeles. It was a no-brainer; I had to accept. Then, Mr. Jones explained the extremely heavy rehearsal schedule, the fact that both works would have to be memorized, and the fee that I would receive: $400. Although this was my big break, I gulped and replied, "I'm sorry. I can't do it for $400."

"Then we'll pay you $600," he said.

"I'll take it." Accepting that job actually cost me around $2,000 in coaching and preparation fees, but it was my major entrance onto the LA music scene. I hired Richard Sheldon, the best Gilbert and Sullivan coach in Los Angeles at the time, and began learning the music, memorizing the dialogue, and working on my British accent. It was a massive task to master the roles of Ralph Rackstraw and Edwin the defendant, but I was determined to deliver and hoped that my coaching investment would be worth it.

After several months of work with Richard, I had my first rehearsal with Roger and the chorale. When I entered the rehearsal room, Robert Willoughby Jones pulled me aside and said, "Roger just fired Byron, one of the long-time choral members. If he yells at you, ignore it." Now that was a real confidence builder. I thought, *Oh no, now what am I in for?*

When we began going through my solos, I was totally "off book," meaning that I had committed both works to memory. From time to time, Roger would look up from his score and nod. Soon, he began asking me about tempos and if I were comfortable with the way that he was conducting the works. I had gone from being petrified by Roger's potential wrath to having him asking me if I wanted anything done differently. From that very first rehearsal with Roger, my stock was on the rise.

Roger was really more interested in the traditional, classical choral works like Bach, Brahms, Haydn, and Beethoven, but he had been talked into doing a couple of nights of Gilbert and Sullivan to widen the Master Chorale's audience and appeal. This Gilbert and Sullivan repertoire didn't carry the gravitas of other more serious classical works.

The subsequent rehearsals and performances on the stage of the Dorothy Chandler Pavilion were a success and led to more solo work with Roger. Shortly thereafter, I was hired to do the tenor solos for the Master Chorale's performance of Haydn's *Harmonie Mass*. It was a nice work and not particularly tough. When I arrived at the one and only rehearsal with the chorale and symphonia, Roger started the orchestra on my solo piece. About two bars after my entrance, he cut off the orchestra and commented in a menacing tone, "You came in wrong." He started the orchestra again, and I began to sing only to have him cut off the symphonia and snarl, "You came in wrong again." With the chorale and symphonia watching, I started sweating, literally and physically. I had no idea what the problem was. We began again and when I entered, he stopped, ripped my score out of my hands, and compared it to his. After checking both of them, he took the eraser on his pencil and erased some markings from his score, and said, "Never mind."

Never mind? The guy had almost given me a heart attack and had embarrassed me in front of some the finest singers and instrumentalists in Los Angeles. Never mind? He started the symphonia again, and I began singing at the same place I had started before. All was well.

Over the years, my friendship with Roger grew. We had great mutual respect for each other. During this time, I was on staff at First Baptist Church of Van Nuys. As I have shared, the extensive music program at the church included the 110-voice Amen Choir. While it was a good choir, these folks were volunteers. Some had a bit of professional training, but most were people who loved to sing and wanted to use their voices to the glory of God. They were a close-knit group, committed to each other and to making music in service to their Savior.

I thought it would be great for the choir members to experience singing for a master conductor like Roger. With some trepidation about what comments might come out of his mouth, I invited him to a Thursday night rehearsal to spend a few moments with the choir.

That particular evening, Roger conducted the choir in the Vivaldi *Gloria in D Major*. At one point, the entrance of the soprano section was disastrous. It was ragged and their pitch was terrible. Roger cut them off and barked, "Sopranos, if you're going to choke, choke together." I laughed out loud and exhaled at the same time. If that was the worst Roger would say, I was relieved. That evening, he was very gracious, and it was a wonderful experience for the choir. It gave them something to talk about for the rest of their choral lives. And it also gave me a great line to use in future rehearsals, "If you're going to choke, choke together."

Steve with conductor Roger Wagner

My final recollection of Roger was the weekend during which I sang in five performances of the *Messiah*: one on Friday night, two on Saturday, and two on Sunday. It was a brutal weekend. After conducting the final performance on Sunday night, Roger was totally spent. He was also in the early stage of cancer. Unless you are a professional, you can't comprehend the demands of conducting the *Messiah* once, let alone five times in one weekend. Following that final performance at the Music Center, Roger needed a ride to his Woodland Hills home. Kristine and I loaded Roger into our blue Volvo and off we went. When we reached his house, I literally helped carry him inside the house because he was so exhausted. He had given every ounce of energy to making Handel's masterpiece come alive. This level of professionalism made working with Roger Wagner a special privilege. Over and over, he showed me that "music gives a soul to the universe, wings to the mind, flight to the imagination, and life to everything."[5]

ENCORE

My favorite tennis professional is known for being extremely limber. He stretches ninety minutes every day, which allows him to make shots that no other player can make. Don't be afraid to stretch beyond your perceived limits. It will help you accomplish things that you never imagined possible.

Chapter Eight

Because of the Brave

"There is no greater love than to lay down one's
life for one's friends."

— John 15:13

From the time I started traveling in 1988, I've flown millions
of miles and sat next to scores of interesting people.
And I've also had my share of bumps along the way. My
"flying partners" have included renowned composer Alan
Menken, tennis great James Blake, and accomplished actor
Joe Mantegna, to mention a few. You never know who you'll
meet when you fly in and out of Los Angeles.

On one flight, I left Burbank Airport for Sacramento to do
a choral workshop with a church choir and to give a concert.
About thirty minutes out, I heard a loud thud and then the
aircraft began to shudder. Terrified, the woman next to me
asked, "What was that?"

"I think we hit a bird and it took out one of our engines,"
I said calmly.

"How many do we have?"

"Well, we had two when we took off."

She was visibly shaken, but I tried to reassure her as we landed in San Jose and transferred to a new aircraft. I'm not sure how successful I was because I don't recall seeing her board the replacement plane to Sacramento. Maybe she took the bus.

On another weekend, I was headed to Savannah, Georgia, to conduct a choral workshop and to sing in the Sunday services at a local church. On the flight from Atlanta to Savannah, I sat next to a gentleman who was reading his church newsletter. We struck up a conversation and exchanged contact information. Little did I know that this divine appointment with Bruce Brereton would be so eventful.

As a high-level executive at Smith-Barney, a major financial services corporation, Bruce was, and still is, a "get-things-done" kind of guy. He served in the Army Special Forces and parachuted out of numerous airplanes as well as conducted special missions in the jungles of El Salvador. And he had the battle scars to back up his stories.

Several months after our airplane encounter, Bruce attended one of my Los Angeles concerts. We stayed in touch, and he continued to ask questions about my ministry.

"Steve," Bruce said, "What do you do, specifically? How do you do it? And how are you organized?" One by one, I answered his questions. Like Bruce, other men and women who have attended my concerts have become members of my board of directors. God has brought a diverse group of people to support me. I love it!

Eventually, I learned that Bruce was connected to the Congressional Medal of Honor Society, a group comprised of heroes who have earned the highest medal that our nation awards: the Medal of Honor. This award is only presented to those who have served in our military. Since its creation, just over 3,500 recipients have earned the medal. Sometimes, people mistakenly refer to them as Medal of Honor winners. But their service wasn't a contest. They didn't win anything. They earned this recognition. A majority of the medals have been awarded posthumously because the recipients paid the ultimate price for their bravery. The lone female recipient is Dr. Mary Walker, who was awarded the medal for caring for soldiers of both sides in the Civil War.

In the fall of 1998, Bruce began talking to me about a Medal of Honor dinner held in the historic dining room at the New York Stock Exchange in NYC. In his typical no-nonsense manner, Bruce set out on his newest mission. He approached his boss, Tom Matthews, co-chairman of the Congressional Medal of Honor Foundation, and said, "Amerson needs to sing at the New York Stock Exchange event."

"I've never heard of the guy. Is he any good?" Tom asked.

"Don't worry about that. I'll take care of getting him there. You just let him sing." Tom acquiesced because arguing with a Special Forces guy is never smart.

I was scheduled to sing "The Star-Spangled Banner" in the elegant ballroom of the NYSE. I didn't have a track for the National Anthem and wanted to do something more than sing a cappella. So I reached out to one of my musician friends, and the two of us crafted a synthesized track to use for the event.

When I arrived at the NYSE, I felt awkward since Bruce had muscled me onto the program, but I trusted that God had put me in the right place at the right time. Surrounded by guests and 125 of America's greatest heroes, I stood on the small stage to open the dinner by singing the National Anthem. I wanted to perform at my personal best. I wanted to "bring it" and not disappoint Bruce.

Before this special event, I asked myself, "If I were a recipient of this award, how would I like to hear 'The Star-Spangled Banner' sung?" So many singers make singing the National Anthem about themselves. Even today my desire is to get out of the way and let the message of a song resonate. That evening when I began to sing, I could sense that I was in a "target-rich environment" and that I was right over the target. As I finished, there was a rousing response and lots of compliments when I made my way back to my table. Bruce was so proud. I was relieved. The recipients were pleased. All was well. That performance opened doors to more Medal of Honor events across the United States. It also allowed me to meet some of the bravest men I will ever know.

After the dinner at the NYSE, I returned to the hotel where all of the Medal of Honor recipients stayed. Some of the recipients, including Tommy Norris and Mike Thornton, invited me to sit with them in the bar and hang. They began telling their stories and I was enthralled. Some of them were even true. These guys knew exactly where and when to embellish so that their tales would hold me captive. Not to mention make me laugh.

When Mike was to receive his medal at the White House, Tommy was in the hospital at Walter Reed. Not to be deterred, Mike had a conversation with Tommy's physician. "Doc, I want Tommy at the White House when the president gives me my medal," Mike said.

"Mike, that's not going to happen," the doctor said.

"Doc, are you listening to me? I want Tommy to be there!"

STEVE AMERSON

"Mike, you're not listening to me. That's not going to happen."

But according to Mike, he rappelled Tommy out of his second-story room at Walter Reed Hospital so that Tommy could be at the White House when Mike received his medal. Whether that's the way it happened or not, it's a great story.

Both Mike and Tommy were awarded the Medal of Honor for their individual acts of valor. Mike's award was presented for saving Tommy's life when Tommy was shot behind enemy lines in North Vietnam. Mike ran through a hail of enemy fire to rescue Tommy, who had taken a round through the temple. Then Mike strapped Tommy and a South Vietnamese soldier to himself and floated in the ocean with both of them for hours until an American ship finally picked them up. In the process of rescuing both men, Mike, too, was shot. If I'm ever in a fight, I want Mike and Tommy on either side of me.

To this day, I consider Tommy and Mike dear friends, even though Mike has sung along with me a few too many times. As I close an event singing "God Bless America," Mike has been known to join me on stage and bellow out the song. Who's going to stop him? He's an American hero. He loves our nation and he loves me.

Sitting in that bar and listening to these men tell their stories was both inspiring and hilarious. In me they found a new audience, and I was royally entertained. After about an hour I was ready to shut down and head to bed. I had an early flight back to Los Angeles the next morning, and I was exhausted. "Hey, Steve," Mike said, "we're headed to another hotel for drinks. You're coming, aren't you?"

How do you say no to a living legend, a former Navy Seal, and a Medal of Honor recipient? But around 2:00 a.m., I gave up and took a taxi back to the Hilton. I have no idea what time Mike called it a night. Or a morning.

Top: Steve with Medal of Honor Recipient, Bruce Crandall.
Bottom: Medal of Honor recipients Leo Thorsness & Mike Thornton with Steve.

After Bruce Brereton opened the door at the NYSE, I continued to get calls from the Medal of Honor Society and Foundation. I also came to know more of the recipients. Although many of them have passed, I remain in touch with some of the living recipients: Gary Beikirch, Pat Brady, Roger Donlan, Sammy Davis, Bruce Crandall, and others hold a special place in my heart. To provide musical material for such events, I created an entire album of patriotic songs titled *Amazed by America*. One of the songs on the CD is "Blades of Grass and Pure White Stones," which my friends Orrin Hatch, Phil Naish, and Lowell Alexander wrote. It has become a favorite of the recipients, and they ask me to sing it at virtually every Medal of Honor event.

In 2009, I was awarded the Bob Hope Award for Excellence in Entertainment from the Medal of Honor Society. Other recipients of this award include Gary Sinise, Jon Voigt, Clint Eastwood, Trace Adkins, Tom Selleck, Bradley Cooper, Tony Orlando and Jay Leno. To become a member of such an esteemed group was humbling.

Since that first performance at the New York Stock Exchange, I have sung for events in numerous cities across the United States as well as onboard the USS Yorktown in Charleston, South Carolina, and at Pearl Harbor in Hawaii. My friendships with the recipients has deepened over the years because they recognize how much I respect the Medal of Honor and how much I love them and respect their service and their sacrifice. To honor the Medal of Honor recipients, my friend, Lowell Alexander, and I wrote the song, "Because of the Brave."

They never asked for glory
They never sought the fame
But they answered the call just the same.
Showing courage beyond duty
With noble, valiant hearts
The flame of freedom shining in the dark.[6]

To view the video of "Because of the Brave," go to www.steveamerson.com/because.

Before Medal of Honor recipient Leo Thorsness passed, I asked him to speak at a worship service in the basement of the United States Capitol. That evening, Leo told about his six years as a prisoner of war in what was called the Hanoi Hilton. On one occasion, the thirty or so prisoners in his cell decided to hold a worship service. They began to pray the Lord's Prayer and as they did, the guards rushed in and dragged the ranking officer out of the cell and began to beat him. They could hear his screams, but they continued to pray. The guards returned and grabbed the next ranking officer out of the cell and began to beat him, but they continued to pray.

This happened several times until Leo was the next prisoner to be removed. But realizing that they couldn't stop the soldiers from praying, the guards gave up. When Leo finished telling his story, he asked us to join him in saying the Lord's Prayer. Standing there with tears streaming down my face, I struggled to utter the prayer as I more deeply understood the price that was paid for our freedom.

Over the years, Bruce Crandall and his wife, Arlene, became great friends of mine. Bruce continues to have a mischievous streak. Whenever I see him, he is always teasing me. He travels with a small dog that he named Huey, and he loves showing off Huey and his tricks like rolling over and sitting up on his haunches. Everywhere he goes, that dog is an attention-getter. As a member of the Army Air Cavalry, Bruce also wears a Stetson hat as part of his uniform. He loves wearing the hat at Medal of Honor events because it sets him apart. He once told me, "It ticks off all the other recipients because I wear this hat." That's Bruce!

The movie *We Were Soldiers* portrayed Bruce's story as an Air Cavalry helicopter pilot. Actor Greg Kinnear played Bruce as the film recounted Bruce's seventeen passes into a dangerous landing zone in the jungles of Vietnam to take out the wounded and to bring in supplies. Even though his superiors ordered Bruce not to do this, he disobeyed to support those on the ground and to rescue the wounded. Bruce and Arlene were on the set of the movie while it was being shot. He said that Greg Kinnear and Mel Gibson stopped by their RV every morning for coffee and a chat.

Bruce shared with me that one of the helicopter crews on his watch went down in the thick jungle vegetation and was never found. Feeling that he was responsible, he carried that weight for over twenty years. When I saw Bruce at one of the Medal of Honor events, he told me that the chopper, a Huey 8808, had been found along with the remains of the crew.

"Steve," Bruce said, "would it be all right if we play a recording of 'Blades of Grass and Pure White Stones' when the remains are buried at Arlington National Cemetery?"

"Of course, Bruce. Please, play the song." There was a long pause.

"Steve," he said, "would you be there in person to sing it?"

"I would be honored. I'll be there when they lay these fine men to rest." And I was. Although years had passed, the crew of Huey 8808 had finally come home. Those brave men would be:

> *Buried here with dignity*
> *Endless rows for all to see,*
> *Freedom's seeds in sorrow sown,*
> *'Neath blades of grass and pure white stones.*[7]

To view the video of "Blades of Grass & Pure White Stones," go to www.steveamerson.com/blades.

Since then, I've sung at several funerals for Medal of Honor recipients, and several living recipients have put in their request for me to sing as well. Several years ago, Bruce's wife, Arlene, died of cancer. When he passes, he will be buried beside her at Arlington National Cemetery. Every time Bruce sees me, he says, "Don't forget. You've promised to be at Arlington to sing 'Blades of Grass and Pure White Stones' when Arlene and I are laid to our final rest."

"I haven't forgotten, Bruce. It will be my privilege to sing for you."

We owe a great debt that we will never be able to repay to these Medal of Honor recipients as well as to all who have served and who now serve the United States of America. Without question, "we are the land of the free because of the brave."

ENCORE

Our lives are filled with people who serve others. Express a word of thanks to a first responder or a veteran today.

CHAPTER NINE

The Three Tenors and "The Three Other Tenors"

"Sing a new song to the LORD! Sing his praises from the ends of the earth. Sing, all you who sail the seas, all you who live in distant coastlands."

— Isa. 42:10

Enrico Caruso, Jussi Bjoerling, and Nicolai Gedda: historic tenors of a bygone era. As a young singer, I listened to the scratchy recordings of their artistry. With the essence of their voices transcending the crude recording techniques of their day, these operatic virtuosos set the standard for years to come.

As time passed, a new generation of exceptional tenors claimed the limelight: Placido Domingo, Jose Carreras, and Luciano Pavarotti. Pavarotti was the most flamboyant and probably the best known. Either he or his manager, maybe both, understood the power of the media to reach the masses. I remember Pavarotti, handkerchief in hand, performing an operatic aria or a Neapolitan song on *The*

Tonight Show and then moving to the couch to engage in banter with Johnny Carson. Audiences loved Pavarotti.

With his larger-than-life personality, Pavarotti expanded the reach of opera to the average listener who would never attend an opera, let alone listen to an operatic aria. In 1990, the three tenors joined forces and sang together in Rome on the eve of the World Cup Soccer Final. An international audience of an estimated 800 million watched the concert on television. The success of that event set in motion The Three Tenors concerts, which continued until 2003. More about that later.

My friend, Ron Hicklin, had an illustrious career as a Los Angeles singer, vocal contractor, and producer. His list of credits is extensive. He sang the opening theme for *Happy Days* as well as for other television shows, movies and recordings. Ever listen to Alvin and the Chipmunks? That's Ron. To produce the sounds of those iconic rodents, Ron recorded at a slow speed and then sped up the tape. "Alvin!" You can also hear Ron's voice on a myriad of other recordings; sometimes, he did the actual singing for groups like The Monkees and The Partridge Family.

Ron had established a stable of phenomenal Los Angeles session singers including Thurl Ravenscroft, the voice of "Tony the Tiger" for Kellogg's Frosted Flakes commercials: "They're Grrrreat!" And Ron's stable of fabulous singers could read music at the speed of light. When I wound up on his radar, he began to use me for movie and television sessions and commercials.

The Hicklin work ethic and standards were daunting, and even though I respected him, I feared him. He wasn't mean, but he cut right to the bone. I remember Ron's starting every session with his standard, "So dig." Then, he gave instructions to the group on vocal approach, tone, cut offs, and whatever else he wanted us to consider. When Ron spoke, everyone listened. I dreaded singing a wrong note or not making the cutoff exactly as he had directed because Ron's ear could detect the slightest mistake.

When I perform as a soloist, I attempt to embrace the moment and make it mine. I bring my style, personality and my interpretation to the song, whether it's classical, pop or Broadway. But as a group singer, my job is to blend with the other voices in a cohesive unit. It's not about me!

In 1990, Ron hired me as part of a twenty-four-voice group to sing on the movie, *The Hunt for Red October*; all of the lyrics were in Russian! As the contractor, Ron's responsibility was to know the stable singers and hire the right voices that could deliver what the producer desired. Ron knew that he could count on me to be a team player and to sing as part of the group, but he also knew that he could request that I step it up and produce a heroic, clarion sound. For this movie score he wanted a robust and dynamic vocal production with lots of bravura akin to the Red Army Chorus.

The five days that we worked on *The Hunt for Red October* were exhilarating and exhausting. Not only did we have to read the music, but with the help of language coaches, we also had to sing the right notes and the correct pronunciation of the words in Russian—on command. The task was less about the beauty or quality of our voices than it was about our ability to focus and to concentrate. Recording passages in a foreign language with percussive consonants at "warp speed" made our heads spin.

At one point in the session, Ron wanted more volume from me and more of the laser-like, cutting edge that my voice could bring. Singing alongside the other tenors in the ensemble, I gave Ron more volume. After he listened to the playback, he asked me to sing louder. Embarrassing? Yeah, definitely. But I dialed it up a notch. The other tenors, all of whom had fine voices, braced themselves for what was coming. We had sung next to each other in previous sessions for years, and we knew what each singer could deliver. After a second take, Ron listened to the playback and then physically moved me closer to the microphone. "Steve, give it to me."

"Okay!" And I gave it all I had, no holding back. Picture that old Memorex commercial: a little guy sits in a chair while the intensity of the speakers blows his hair and scarf back like a hurricane!

When the film was released several months later, Kristine and I went to see it. As the opening scene began to unfold, a dramatic mix of singing and orchestration filled the theater. Soon, the voices of the Russian sailors onboard the submarine were at maximum force. Hearing my full-throated voice louder than any others, Kristine gave me a knowing look. Ron got what he wanted.

In 1994, Ron called with a special project. This time he wanted me to sing some demos for Luciano Pavarotti. Ron explained that The Three Tenors were going to do a concert at Dodger Stadium, which would include operatic arias but also medley arrangements of popular songs created by musician and movie composer Lalo Shiffrin. Famous for composing the *Mission Impossible* theme, Lalo was a classical and jazz musician who would bring creative arrangements to The Three Tenors performances.

The producer of the concert asked to have Lalo's medley arrangements recorded so that Pavarotti could learn his part. It's hard to believe that one of the finest tenors in the world didn't know how to read music. With Lalo's full orchestration of the first medley reduced to a piano score, I went into the studio with a pianist, an engineer, and Ron to record the three vocal parts of Pavarotti, Domingo, and Carreras. As the producer, Ron employed a technique known as overdubbing: I sang one track and then a second and then a third. Ron and the engineer took those tracks and did a quick mix of my singing all three tenor parts. Although the response to my demo was positive, the tenors wanted three different voices so that they could tell when their part was being sung. Here we go again!

To accommodate the stars request, Ron added Augustino Castagnola and Jonathan Mack to the team. Fellow tenors and friends, Augie and Jon and I knew each other from the studios and the concert world. "The Three Other Tenors," as we called ourselves, stepped into the studio and recorded the demonstration tracks for the upcoming Los Angeles concert. It took weeks. Although the work was lengthy and painstaking, the final product, which an audience would never hear, gave the tenors exactly what they needed. Over the next twelve years, we "three other tenors" sang demo tapes in multiple languages for The Three Tenors' concerts. We had a pretty good grasp of Latin, Spanish, and French and, of course, we all knew English. Augie guided us through the Italian songs and Jon, fresh from working in Germany, coached us in German. Additional coaches assisted us in Russian, Portuguese, Japanese, and Korean.

Top: Jonathan Mack, Augie Castagnola, Ron Hicklin, Lalo Schriffin, and Steve
Bottom: Steve, Jonathan, Lalo, and Augie

Of all the sessions I've ever done, recording these demos was the most demanding. It required reading and singing the correct notes and words on pitch and with some type of artistic style to inspire the "real" tenors. After a full day of performing at a microphone, I went home physically and emotionally exhausted. The flip side was that creating these demos was some of the most satisfying work I've ever done because it required all of my training and artistry.

Finally, the weekend of the Los Angeles concert arrived. On Friday afternoon, Augie, Jon, and I were invited to the first of two rehearsals at Dodger Stadium. Initially, the producer told us that we would sing the first rehearsal with the Los Angeles Philharmonic Orchestra and the Los Angeles Music Center Opera Chorus under the baton of Maestro Zubin Mehta. Then, we heard that one of the tenors would sing at the rehearsal. Not to be outdone, the other two tenors also decided to show up. Augie, Jon, and I appeared as requested and had a brief moment with the "real" tenors before the rehearsal began. At that rehearsal, Domingo complimented me on the rehearsal tracks I had prepared for him. While we weren't given tickets to the actual performance, we were invited to attend the final dress rehearsal that evening to hear the way that our work had assisted The Three Tenors in preparing for the concert. While watching that final dress rehearsal, we realized that the event would be a spectacular visual and aural experience.

The next day, Saturday July 16, 1994, The Three Tenors sang to a packed Dodger Stadium as Kristine and I watched on television from our den. No one knew that I had even played a part in one of the most significant classical musical events in the history of the world. For those who would like to know more, *The Making of the Three Tenors* concert video can be found on YouTube. Augie, Jon and I are included in that documentary. To view the video *The Making of the Three Tenors* concert, go to www.steveamerson/threetenors.

What we thought was a one-time job developed into more work in the coming years. Once again, Ron Hicklin summoned us to assist the tenors in preparing for a 1996 concert in New York City and for a 1998 concert in Paris. Augie, Jon and I joked about using the arrangements that we had learned and recorded and presenting concerts as "The Other Three Tenors." Of course, we wouldn't have packed out Dodger Stadium.

In 2002, Augie, Jon and I were contacted to see if we would prepare demo recordings for a future concert in Yokohama, Japan. Only this time, Ron Hicklin didn't call us. Thinking that they could save money, the production company contacted us directly and asked us to record the demos. Augie, Jon, and I discussed the invitation and declined. Since Ron Hicklin was the contractor who initially brought the work to us, we thought it was inappropriate to accept if he were not included. I called Ron to explain what was happening. "We don't feel right about this," I said. "You're the one who brought us to this party so we told them no."

"Steve," Ron replied, "you guys are three talented, stand-up tenors. And I'm grateful for your loyalty. Take the work, with my blessing."

We took the work, and as it turned out, I became the producer of the demonstration recordings for the concert, which was targeted to a Japanese and Korean audience. It meant that in addition to singing, I would also hire Augie and Jon, book the studio and engineer, hire the pianist and the language coach to help us sing in Japanese and Korean. My years of experience in singing and producing my own recording projects had equipped me for the challenge of preparing demos for three of the greatest tenors in history.

Singing and producing the demonstration tapes for The Three Tenors remains a high point of my career. Think about it. How many singers can say that they gave musical instruction to Luciano Pavarotti?

ENCORE

Sometimes we are called to serve in the background. Others may get all the applause and adulation. God sees. God knows.

CHAPTER TEN

Standing over a Hot Mic

"And now, dear brothers and sisters, one final thing. Fix your thoughts on what is true, and honorable, and right, and pure, and lovely, and admirable. Think about things that are excellent and worthy of praise."

— Phil. 4:8

Few things make you feel more vulnerable than standing alone at a microphone in a studio while being recorded. The engineer on the other side of the glass can hear every imperfection. It's like being under an aural microscope, and the playback can be brutal when you hear the raw sound of your voice. I've spent hundreds of hours in front of the microphone to try and capture the optimum performance. Not the perfect performance—the optimum performance. There are times when a less-than-perfect performance may communicate more emotion than a "perfect" one. This recording process is exhausting and exhilarating at the same time.

When I was in high school, I began trying my hand at recording myself using a simple Aiwa mono reel-to-reel tape recorder. I don't have any of those original recordings and that's probably best. In college, I was exposed to more technically advanced recording equipment like a TEAC four-track reel-to-reel recorder. It can't compare with today's digital technology, which is faster and allows for an almost infinite number of tracks. At the time I had no idea that I would become an expert in the recording process.

A few years after arriving in Los Angeles, I made some demo recordings for a publishing company with a highly accomplished trio comprised of producer, Paul Stilwell, engineer, Toby Foster, and arranger, Bob Krogstad. Those three men would influence my career for years to come.

In 1982, I made my first professional solo recording of a Christmas song that I co-wrote with my friend, Paul Johnson. In college, I had heard a recording of Paul's a capella arrangements of songs by John W. Peterson. The sound that Paul created with voices was stunning. I listened to that cassette tape over and over as I traveled in my yellow Dodge Colt. Never could I have imagined that I would write songs with Paul, or that he would become a close friend.

With some orchestral tracks that we previously recorded in London, I stood in front of a microphone in a tiny booth at Cherokee Studios in Los Angeles to record the vocals for two songs: "Is There a Place?" which Paul and I wrote and "Emmanuel" which Ron Gollner composed. With Toby engineering and Paul Stilwell producing, the recording process touched something deep within me. Feeling as if I belonged, I said to myself, "I can do this." I was hooked.

Under the tutelage of these friends, I learned the ins and outs of recording. They taught me the literal punching in and out of tracks. Using headphones to hear myself on an earlier pass, I would sing along. During this process, Toby would punch the record button to capture a word or phrase and then would deftly punch out of record at just the right time. In those days we recorded on two-inch tape. Today, the process would be done using a computer and typically using a program called ProTools. In addition to learning how to record my solo vocals, I learned how to record instruments, create budgets, collaborate with arrangers, book recording studios and engineers, hire instrumentalists and background singers, and a myriad of other production techniques.

After creating my first five solo recordings using that production team, I struck out on my own, producing my solo projects with additional engineers and arrangers. Along the way, I sometimes made mistakes, which expanded my knowledge and wisdom. But sometimes a mistake wreaked havoc with my budget. I caught on quickly and began including a cushion of ten or fifteen percent to allow for unexpected expenses.

One time, I hired an arranger that I had only used once before. This guy was a brilliant arranger and orchestrator with a huge list of film credits. I was concerned about getting into a rut and wanted to be open to new ideas and collaborators. But he was the wrong arranger for that particular song. When he handed me the score and I listened to the synth mock-up, I knew I had hired the wrong guy. What he had created didn't fit the song, and his orchestral background wouldn't communicate the song's message. After paying him for his work, I called the dependable Bob Krogstad, who delivered a stunning orchestration of "Kyrie," a song my friend, Bill Cantos and I composed. Bobby nailed it.

Dismissing the first arranger wasn't fun, but he did get paid. On one other occasion, I hired the wrong drummer. Mind you, this drummer was a "first call" drummer in Los Angeles and a friend, but he was the wrong guy for the style of the songs I was recording. Walking from the control room to the drum booth and letting him go was hard, really hard. This musician was a friend and he wanted to deliver for me, but he knew I was right. It strained our relationship for a brief time but eventually we mended the rift.

Over the years, I worked at a studio in North Hollywood built by the legendary Bill Schnee. I don't use the word legendary lightly. Bill was an engineer and mixer who worked with superstar musicians: Natalie Cole, Bette Midler, Johnny Mathis, Barry Manilow, Barbra Streisand, and a host of others. With the assistance of Toby Foster, Bill created a studio at 4166 Lankershim Boulevard that was a magical place. The studio's custom-made mixing board, state-of-the-art electronic gear, and a host of vintage microphones were unmatched. And with Bill in the engineer's chair, the setup was as close to perfect as one could imagine.

Around 2005, I began the pre-production work on my *Sacred Spaces* project, a collection of sacred songs in six different languages but with a modern twist. I thought about asking Bill Schnee to produce and engineer the project with me. I stood in awe of Bill. Although I had seen him from time to time at his studio, I was hesitant to engage with him. He was out of my league.

Finally, I found the courage to call Bill and ask if he might work with me. I distinctly recall that day. When I arrived at the studio, Bill was in the middle of mixing a song. I slipped into the back of the room and sat quietly while Bill worked his magic by putting every instrument and every note into its proper place within the arrangement. He started and stopped over and over as he made precise adjustments on the faders on the handcrafted mixing board that stretched before him. At one point he yelled, "You idiot." I was shocked! I thought, "Uh oh. This meeting isn't getting off to a great start." Oblivious as to what I had done wrong, I quietly said, "I'm sorry."

"I'm not talking to you. I'm talking to myself," he barked. I soon learned that Bill had high expectations not only of those he worked with but also of himself. That made me want to work with him all the more. Excellence!

When Bill reached a place in the mixing process where he could take a break, we went to a nearby Starbucks to talk. What I didn't know was that Bill held me in high esteem because I had made good on a debt to his studio from years earlier. I was unaware that there was an outstanding balance from a previous project recorded at his studio. When I found out about the debt, I wrote Bill a letter and promised to pay the debt as quickly as I could. I kept my promise. To this day Bill says, "Steve, you ruined a string of Christian musicians who didn't keep their word."

Over coffee, I described the project that I wanted to create with Bill's help. At one point, he asked what kind of a budget I had. When I told him he said, "I don't know how to work with a budget that small."

I started back-peddling. "Bill, I get it. And I really appreciate your meeting with me."

"I didn't say I wouldn't work with you," Bill responded.

That meeting started a working relationship and a deep friendship that remains solid to this day.

Singing in his studio was an absolute joy. The acoustics of the room summoned the voice from inside me so that singing was nearly effortless. Not only were the technical elements of the room first class, but while the room was under construction Bill laid on the concrete floors and prayed for the space. Virtually every instrumentalist and singer who worked in the studio knew that there was something extraordinary, even spiritual, about recording there.

Bill Schnee and Steve at Schnee Studios

Bill taught me to go for the emotion rather than strive for vocal perfection. A crack in my voice or a being a touch out of tune might communicate the emotion of a lyric in a powerful way. I learned to trust Bill, and he began to pull performances out of me that I never could have done on my own. On my *Front Row Center II* project I recorded "We Can Be Kind," a wonderful song by David Freidman that speaks to the importance of being kind and gracious to others. At one point, Bill could hear the imperfection in my vocal performance because of the way that the lyric touched me. Rather than make it perfect, Bill advised me to leave it. He was right.

Over the years and seven different projects, Bill and I developed an intense recording style. It's pretty simple. I shut up and sing and he records. It works for me and really works for him. If I make a mistake, I hear it. Bill hears it. We don't need to discuss it because it would be a waste of time. If Bill hears something he thinks can be better, he simply stops recording, rewinds and starts again to pick up the word or phrase that needs to be replaced. No explanation necessary. As soon as I hear the track, I start singing full out and we press on. Bill often says that he is exhausted after recording me for several hours because there is so little down time. Like *Star Trek* characters, our minds meld.

As a producer Bill also goes for the emotion. He has become "second ears" to my voice and my heart. I know that my artistry and my heart are safe with him. There have been times when I've been emotionally overwhelmed in the midst of recording because of the content of the lyric or the beauty of a melody. Bill simply stops recording, gives me a moment to recover and then we press on. This has happened on several occasions including when I recorded the song, "Kyrie," from my *Sacred Spaces* CD. The lyric combined with Bob Krogstad's orchestration brought me to tears.

When Bill relocated to Nashville, it was a tough good-bye. No more could we have those weekly lunches to discuss music, family, careers, and our shared faith. Even though he now lives outside Music City, he's still my first choice for an engineer. When we work together, we easily slip back into our artist and engineer roles. I sing. He records. Talking is not necessary.

If a song impacts me, I trust that it will impact the listener. I can normally tell the first time I hear a song. Several years ago, Pastor Scott Bauer said, "Steve, every song you sing is like a sermon." That is my intention—to compose and to select songs for recording and performing that have deep lyrical content blended with melodies that support and amplify the lyrics. Then, I try to get out of the way so that the words and the melody pierce the heart of the audience. As a person of faith, I believe that God's Spirit resides in me. When I exhale as I sing, I envision the Holy Spirit's transporting the words and the melody from inside me to the listener so that the words touch the heart with beauty and truth. I am so blessed to stand at the mic on stages and in studios around the world and offer God's gift: my voice.

ENCORE

Find and work with people who believe in you and want to help you be your best. And be someone who brings out the best in others.

CHAPTER ELEVEN

Live from Carnegie Hall

"Don't worry about anything; instead, pray about
everything. Tell God what you need, and thank
him for all he has done."

— Phil. 4:6

Virtually every musician aspires to perform at Carnegie
Hall—the pinnacle of concert venues. On two occasions, I've had the honor to perform on that stage. The first
time was April 24, 2006, when I was the tenor soloist in the
premier of a work titled, *Missa Americana*. Composed by Ed
Lojeski, the composition combined the classical mass form
with American musical styles while incorporating English
and traditional Latin texts.

Another Los Angeles session singer had recommended
me to sing on the demonstration recording of this new work
for the publisher. Doing this recording gave Ed a chance to
hear my voice and opened the opportunity for me to sing at
the New York City premiere.

Ed Lojeski was well known for his composing and arrang-
ing works for school choirs. There's probably not a high

school choir in the United States that hasn't performed at least one of Ed's arrangements. While most of Ed's arrangements were of popular and contemporary songs, *Missa Americana* was his opportunity to make his mark in the more classical genre of choral music. The work was a contemporary mass, hence the name "Missa," and included modern jazz idioms merged with a classical approach. It was written in five movements. I was the soloist in the fourth movement, the "Offertory." I also sang a duet with the soprano soloist in the fifth movement, the "Sanctus and Benedictus"; in the final movement, the "Agnus Dei," the soprano and I sang with the chorus.

I enjoyed my portion of the composition because while it was contemporary, it was more melodic than works like Stravinsky's *Canticum Sacrum, Symphony of Psalms, Oedipus Rex, Les Noces,* or other modern works that I had performed. Ed's composition style was accessible to the average listener.

The orchestra for the performance consisted of New York professionals; the choir was an assemblage of high school and amateur adult singers from around the country. They were singers who were familiar with Ed's work and thrilled to be included in this premiere at Carnegie Hall. Part of the fun of that performance was that one of the daughters of close friends, Chris and Jina Virtue, was in the choir. Early in my career, Chris and Jina had nicknamed me MOGO: "Man of God and Opera." They had also attended my performances at the Hollywood Bowl and other Southern California venues. But that evening, they were on the other coast where they heard their daughter perform as well as shared in my Carnegie Hall debut. It was a "two-fer."

My solo movement, "Offertory," was based on Philippians 4:6 and Psalm 138. As I stood on that Carnegie Hall stage for the first time, the words that came from my lips were the scripture, "Be anxious for nothing." With great intent I proclaimed those words. As I applied my years of training from my mentor Alan Rogers Lindquest, my voice resonated throughout the hall. With some years of experience and maturity, I was not gripped by the fear that I had felt years earlier at the Hollywood Bowl. On that night in Carnegie Hall I was in my sweet spot.

My desire was to let those words from Philippians and Psalm 138 pierce the hearts of those in the audience who may have been dealing with a multitude of fears. For me, it was not just about performing; it was about using my voice to breathe life into them and to fill the hall. As I relished my first foray into the Carnegie Hall venue, I felt as if I belonged.

My second opportunity to perform at Carnegie Hall was with two other well-known Christian tenors, Steve Green and Larnelle Harris. The concert was on October 18, 2011. Ten years earlier, the three of us had sung together at Bass Hall in Fort Worth, Texas. Tickets for those two concerts sold out in one day. My close friend, Paul Stilwell, helped organize the concert, which Christian music legend, Ralph Carmichael conducted. Steve and Larnelle have long and respected careers in gospel music and to sing again with these two respected tenors was an honor. Although they had sung together on numerous occasions, we three tenors had only sung together that one time in Fort Worth.

The Carnegie Hall concert featured each of us performing some of our signature solos as well as singing several trio numbers. The trios included selections from Greg

Nelson's work, *Saviour,* and the beloved hymn, "It Is Well with My Soul." A choir made up of members from around the United States and a magnificent orchestra, all under David Hamilton's direction, rounded out the concert. Longtime friend, Dick Tunney, who had worked with all three tenors before, was at the piano. Dick built his reputation on song-writing as well as his work accompanying Steve Green and Sandi Patty.

Steve, Larnelle Harris, and Steve Green at Carnegie Hall

My solo selections for the concert included, "This Must Be the Place," a song that I composed with my friend Cary Schmidt. This song reminds the church that it must be a place of grace—that evening, Carnegie Hall became a place that proclaimed God's grace.

What distinguished me from Steve and Larnelle was the wealth of Broadway selections in my repertoire. Years earlier my friend, Chuck Swindoll, said, "Steve, you need to sing 'Bring Him Home' in your concerts." When Chuck Swindoll, a respected pastor and prolific author, made a suggestion, you took it.

Chuck was right. Including that Broadway "secular" number had as much impact in my church concerts as the "Christian" songs. It caused me to re-evaluate the way that I defined not only my songs but also my daily activities. Too often we separate the sacred from the secular. It's easy to say that a pastor's job is sacred whereas a mechanic's job is secular. Nothing could be further from the truth. Each of us can do what we do as our ministry. I often encouraged my friend and radio personality, Rick Dees, to play those Top 40 hits as his ministry so that his voice would impact millions of listeners each morning on the radio. With his distinctive style, Rick made occasional mentions of his faith and used his place behind the microphone to be an encourager to his worldwide listening audience. He demonstrated that we don't have to bombard people with the plan of salvation to impact their lives and move them closer to God.

For my other two solo selections at Carnegie Hall, I sang, "Bring Him Home" from the musical, *Les Miserables,* and "Into the Fire" from the musical, *The Scarlet Pimpernel.* Both songs have intense spiritual meaning, especially *Les Miserables,* a story of the way that God showed grace to Jean Valjean and the way Valjean shared that grace with others.

My Carnegie Hall appearances were consistent with the direction the board of Amerson Ministries had established years earlier. They encouraged me to sing in all types of venues: churches, corporate situations, and symphony concerts. They also approved the creation of a recording titled *Front Row Center,* an album comprised entirely of inspirational Broadway and movie songs. The creation of this recording and the subsequent *Front Row Center: II* CD opened new doors of opportunity, including singing some of those songs at Carnegie Hall.

Several years before this concert with Steve and Larnelle, I met some New York City firefighters through my friend and well-known actor, Gary Sinise. Gary is one of the kindest men you will ever meet. Following the tragedy of 9/11, Gary became friends with many of the firefighters who fought so ferociously that day. Since September 11, 2001, Gary has given of himself to support our troops, military families, and first responders. His Gary Sinise Foundation is dedicated to those who serve.

The day before we three tenors performed at Carnegie Hall, some of my firefighter friends escorted Kristine and me to Ground Zero and then to a memorial dedicated to those who died on 9/11. It was humbling for these men to lead us to the place filled with so much heartache.

The producer of the concert provided complimentary tickets, which I shared with my New York City Fire Department friends. That night before I sang "Into the Fire," I asked fifty of New York City's finest to stand and be recognized. While it was a privilege to sing in Carnegie Hall, the greater privilege was honoring these men and women. They were the ones who "faced the valley, rallied to win, and never held back for a moment." Truly, they were the ones who rushed "into the fire."[8]

ENCORE

An old joke asks: "How to you get to Carnegie Hall? Practice." I practiced but I also followed my heart. Where is your heart leading you? What great thing is God calling you to accomplish?

CHAPTER TWELVE

Ministering to the Ministers

"And how will anyone go and tell them without being sent? That is why the Scriptures say, 'How beautiful are the feet of messengers who bring good news.'"

— Rom. 10:15

I've had the privilege to work with many distinguished pastors and authors, three of whom hold special places in my heart: Chuck Swindoll, David Jeremiah, and Jack Hayford.

In the early 1990s, I received an invitation to provide music for a family camp with Insight for Living (IFL) at Mount Hermon in the Santa Cruz Mountains of Northern California. Insight for Living was the radio and publishing ministry of pastor and author Chuck Swindoll. The invitation was special because I admired Chuck and his work. He was a phenomenal Bible teacher as well as loads of fun, so down-to-earth, and unafraid to laugh at a joke or at himself. It made him human and opened people's hearts to his message.

Since it was summer, all four Amersons went to the Mount Hermon Family Camp for a week. During the morning, the children and teens enjoyed multiple games and activities while the adults listened to great speakers and Bible teachers. In the evening everyone met together for music, loony contests, and games, after which Chuck delivered an inspirational message.

Even though I was new to Chuck and Cynthia Swindoll and the IFL family, they greeted me warmly. They also recognized that I loved a good laugh. While Chuck was the message and the heart of IFL, Cynthia was the COO (Chief Operational Officer). Her keen eye and organizational skills were top notch, and she and Chuck made an impressive team.

One evening, Chuck and Cynthia's son, Curt, asked me to participate in a prank on Chuck. I was usually up for anything, and since this was the fifth of seven nights of meetings, Curt didn't want to miss this chance. In only five days, I had learned that the entire IFL team loved to laugh, tell jokes, and generally cut loose. The crowning achievement was to cause Chuck to laugh and howl only as he could. That sound was somewhere between a goat call and a giant sneeze. Sometimes, people just laughed at Chuck's laughter.

Even though we were both in our thirties, Curt and I were still ornery preachers' kids. Having grown up in the Swindoll family, Curt knew the craziness that could ensue. His proposition was simple.

"Steve, in the opening segment of tonight's meeting, you and will I act like we're having a fight. You chase me with a pie tin filled with whipped cream. When we get near my dad, I'll stop and instead of hitting me in the face with the whipped cream, you hit my dad. He'll love it. He'll think it's a hoot, and all the people attending the camp will love it."

I had my misgivings, but Curt assured me his dad would be a good sport. In the few short days I had known Curt, I had grown to trust him. Hit Chuck Swindoll with a pie? What could go wrong?

Right on cue, Curt and I started our routine as he ran around the room. He headed for his dad and as planned, he ducked and I nailed Chuck in the face with the whipped cream pie. Everyone loved it and laughed heartily. What I didn't know was that Chuck was wearing a brand-new jean jacket that a publisher had just given him. The jacket had an embroidered logo—very cool until whipped cream was smeared onto it. Chuck was gracious and played along, but I could tell by the look on Cynthia's face that she was less than pleased. To this day, I can't believe that I did that. But I must admit, the fact that I hit Chuck with a pie may have solidified my participation in future events. They liked what I brought musically and spiritually; plus the entire team saw that I wasn't afraid to have fun.

Grace is a wonderful thing and that week at Mount Hermon led to a lasting friendship and working relationship with Chuck and Cynthia. Over the years, I sang for Insight For Living events across the United States as well as in Israel, Canada, and Australia. And just think—I could have ruined everything with a whipped cream pie.

We continued to laugh our way around the United States and abroad. IFL held many of its events in large churches and arenas. Ever popular, Chuck drew crowds of ten to twelve thousand. I led the congregational singing and sang solos in many of these large events and for cruises and tours.

Chuck owned a Harley Davidson motorcycle, and in some arenas after he was introduced, he rode that Harley right onto the stage. The crowd went wild. It set the tone for the program because people knew that it would not only be a night of inspiration but also a night of fun. After his grand entrance, Chuck introduced me, and I pedaled to the stage on a tricycle. More laughter! That's what I got for hitting Chuck in the face with a pie.

After some years of relatively "smooth sailing," Kristine and I faced a big challenge. In 1994, our home sustained major damage in the Northridge earthquake. Although we were rebuilding, we were apprehensive about our future. We strongly considered selling our home and moving to Nashville. In fact, we were pretty sure that was what God had in store for us. Just as the deal neared completion, the buyers backed out. Now what? We thought we heard God telling us to make a move. The earthquake was devastating enough, topped now by additional disappointment.

Around that time, I sang for an IFL event in Scottsdale, Arizona. In a few private moments with Chuck, I said, "We go through the earthquake and our home sustains over $150,000 in damage. A door opens to sell our house and move on and then the door is slammed. I'm ticked at God."

Without judgment or condescension, Chuck said, "It's okay. God can handle it." That night Chuck taught me a lesson. It's okay to be mad at God and okay to tell Him. Actually, He already knows. Chuck has written many books and preached a myriad of sermons on grace. I've also seen him live it.

Chuck Swindoll and Steve

Without our knowing it, IFL reached out to some of their supporters who knew us and collected funds to assist us in our $12,000 deductible in repairing our home. We were totally surprised and very grateful. Although the project took over a year, the repairs finally happened. During this time our family lived in a hotel for about four months and in a rental house for an additional six months. The entire experience deepened our faith. God is good, all the time.

My number-one memory was onboard a sailing ship with Chuck and Cynthia and a group of IFL supporters. It was a dream trip for Kristine and me and it happened to be our twenty-third wedding anniversary. We visited the Greek Isles with stops in Athens, Istanbul, Patmos, Kudasi, Rhodes, and Santorini. Each evening before Chuck spoke, I sang.

After one particularly beautiful day on the island of Santorini, we returned to the ship for an elegant meal on deck. Following dinner, I stood on the deck and presented a concert of Broadway songs underneath a moonlit sky with the city lights of Santorini surrounding us. The food, the weather, and setting were spectacular. When I hit the final notes of "You'll Never Walk Alone," the captain of the ship unfurled the sails and we sailed out of the bay. It was magical. And as we continued our Aegean Sea journey, we were not "alone." To this day whenever I see Chuck, all I have to say is "Santorini"—nothing more—and we both smile. It was a stunning evening and a singular memory.

Another respected author and pastor with whom I traveled was David Jeremiah. Our most memorable trip was to Israel. David led a tour of about 400 folks, and we toured the major historical sites that followers of Jesus expect to see. At various sites our group held meetings: in boats on the Sea of Galilee, in the Garden Tomb, and on the Southern Steps just outside the city walls of Jerusalem. One morning, we gathered on those steps, and I sang a song that I had co-written titled, "This Could Be The Day." As I stood there and sang near the walls surrounding the old city of Jerusalem, it struck me that perhaps that morning might actually be the day that Christ returned. What better place to meet the Lord than in Jerusalem.

This could be the day
That the Lord returns in glory
This could be the day
That He calls His children home
So be faithful in service

STEVE AMERSON

As you watch and pray
For this, oh this
This could be the day.[9]

To hear Steve sing "This Could be the Day," go to www. steveamerson/thiscouldbe.

Singing at events for David Jeremiah on the road as well as at his church in El Cajon, California, was always a joy. His preaching was solid, and he showed me that he was truly a person of grace. I experienced this in the way that he treated others, including me, whenever any of us made a silly misstep.

When Kristine and I moved to California and learned of Pastor Jack Hayford. He pastored a church a mile east of the First Baptist Church of Van Nuys where I had come to work. Pastor Jack was well respected and quite a preacher. In 1995, we began to attend The Church on The Way and got to know Pastor Jack and his wife, Anna.

Pastor Jack was one of those preachers who could preach for an hour, sometimes more, and the time would fly. While sitting under Pastor Jack's teaching, we learned so much about how God still works among His people. The power that brought Jesus out of the tomb is still available to believers today. Grace also was a firm part of Pastor Jack's ministry. When pastors of other theological persuasions were critical of Pastor Jack, I saw him respond gracefully and set a powerful, loving example of how to deal with criticism.

In addition to being an outstanding preacher, Pastor Jack had a worldwide reputation. He founded the Jack Hayford School of Pastoral Nurture, a five-day experience offered ten times each year in which pastors of various denominations from around the world traveled to southern California to learn from him. As our friendship grew, Pastor Jack said, "Steve, Anna and I are going to be hosting these pastors for an evening at our home. And we'd like to do something special. Would you come over on Tuesday night and present a concert for these men and women?"

So for more than twelve years on a Tuesday evening, I loaded up my sound gear and drove to the Hayford home. Pastor Jack and Anna provided a scrumptious barbecue dinner for the attendees. After spending the entire day teaching these pastors, Pastor Jack and Anna enjoyed a few moments having dinner while the pastors sat outside and enjoyed the food and the California weather. On every occasion, Jack and Anna invited Kristine and me to eat and chat with them at the kitchen table.

Looking back, I realize the value of those dinners. We talked about so many subjects: raising children, leading a church, telling funny stories. Anna took great joy in giving me grief, but I gave it right back to her. I would sometimes ask why my picture wasn't on the refrigerator along with their family pictures. She would always give me some lame excuse. One night, I brought an 11x17 poster of myself and put it on the refrigerator. "Anna, now you can think of me every time you open the refrigerator."

She responded with some remark about how my picture on the refrigerator might help her with her diet. Pastor Jack leaned back, smiled, and enjoyed the banter. Those two people fed not only my body but also my soul. Following dinner, I would stand in their living room and sing for the forty or so pastors. In all, I sang at over 150 of these events.

Pastor Jack knew my repertoire and often selected the songs for me to sing. He loved it when I sang Broadway selections like "Bring Him Home" or "Into the Fire" because he wanted the pastors to think broadly about innovative ways to reach people. He taught these pastors that God can use anything, even a secular song, to touch the human heart.

At one point, I began to struggle with my faith regarding some personal disappointments. Pastor Jack invited me over, and we sat in the living room for four hours and talked. "Pastor Jack," I said, "if there is a God, I think He's forgotten my name."

"Steve," he said, "sometimes we go through things so we might know God's heart. The real question is not who is God and how does He operate? But who is Steve Amerson and how does he operate?" His words, spoken without judgment but with love and compassion, cut me to the core. It was a turning point. So many times it's easier to look to outward circumstances that impact our lives rather than to look inward. A friend of mine once told me: "Don't tell God what you need. Tell Him what you have."

Scripture is clear that the more we experience suffering, the more our faith deepens and the more we understand the heart of God. 1 Peter 4:12–13, reminds us:

> Beloved, do not think it strange concerning
> the fiery trial which is to you, as though some
> strange thing happened to you; but rejoice to
> the extent that you partake of Christ's sufferings,
> that when His glory is revealed, you may also be
> glad with exceeding joy.

Bottom line: If you want to get closer to God, you will go through suffering. Out of those precious moments with Pastor Jack, I wrote the lyric to "The Father's Heart."

> *That I might know the Father's heart*
> *That I might follow in His ways*
> *It is my prayer to be a servant set apart*
> *To always trust Him and obey*
> *That I might know the Father's heart*
> *That I might somehow share His pain*
> *And in my death to self I'll know in greater part*
> *The awesome glory of His name.*[10]

To hear Steve sing "The Father's Heart," go to www.steveamerson.com/thefathersheart.

On numerous occasions Kristine has stated that while these "giants of the faith" encouraged me, I ministered to the ministers because my singing inspired them before they preached the Word. They were a grace to me and I was a grace to them.

ENCORE

Everyone you know has a battle or a challenge that you know nothing about. Someone around you, even someone in leadership is in need of encouragement. Be a "Barnabas" (an encourager) today.

CHAPTER THIRTEEN

A Voice on the Hill

"Everyone must submit to governing authorities. For all authority comes from God, and those in positions of authority have been placed there by God."

— Rom. 13:1

In 2014, a new avenue opened when a friend shared with me that after an absence of 144 years, weekly worship services would be re-established in the United States Capitol. From 1800 to 1869, weekly worship services were held in Statuary Hall, which at that time was the House Chamber. The room was often filled to capacity with Sunday worshippers. When he was president, Thomas Jefferson rode his horse from the White House to the Capitol to attend these services. Local pastors from around the city preached at this nondenominational gathering, which often included the Marine Corps band playing for the hymns. Thomas Jefferson's complaints were that the singing wasn't fervent enough and that the sermons were too short. Unlike Thomas Jefferson, many of today's church attendees can't wait for the sermon to be over.

At the invitation of my friend, on Wednesday night July 30, 2014, Kristine and I joined a small group of believers to reestablish these services in the United States Capitol. It was our thirty-seventh wedding anniversary. What a way to celebrate. I was asked to sing and lead worship at this inaugural service in Room HC5 in the Capitol basement. This room is used for congressional gatherings in which lawmakers discuss legislation and strategy. Lobbyists also use the room to host receptions and to engage with members of Congress. This would be my first time to lead an event in the Capitol, and I was in awe of stepping into this amazing space. Years later, I'm still in awe.

That first service was filled with singing and preaching and recounting the historical significance of our gathering. I remember one member of Congress passionately praying for God's blessing and guidance in that inaugural service. In attendance were a couple of members of Congress. Any outside group meeting in the Capitol must have at least one member of Congress present.

Following our service, we made our way to the second floor of the Capitol and entered the Rotunda, the most significant and sacred space in the entire building. With the eight gigantic frescos on the walls surrounding us and the dome with the Apotheosis of Washington above, a sense of wonder overcomes those who enter this amazing space. You can almost feel the presence of our Founding Fathers. Even though I've been in this room hundreds of times since then, I still feel the majesty of that space. How privileged I am to stand in the Rotunda. And how blessed I am to lift my voice and sing in this room.

That evening we gathered at the center of the room around what is known as The Golden Circle. From this point on the floor, the streets of Washington, DC, were originally laid out like spokes of a wheel. Standing there gives you the feeling that you are at the heart of our nation. Some have likened it to being in the "holy of holies" of the United States. And many are unaware that adjacent to the Rotunda on the west side is a prayer chapel for members of Congress that President Eisenhower established. It is a small room that can hold twenty people max with a stained-glass window that depicts a kneeling George Washington. It's been my privilege to speak and to sing in that chapel numerous times.

People who question the "separation of church and state" and wonder how worship can take place in the Capitol don't understand the history behind those words. I should also point out that numerous religions have held services on Capitol Hill and in the Capitol for decades.

Many believe that Thomas Jefferson was a deist but in the front of his Bible he wrote the words, "I am a real Christian, that is to say, a disciple of the doctrines of Jesus."[11] Regardless, Jefferson, a man of deep conviction, wrote a letter to the Danbury Baptist Association in 1802 that contains the phrase "wall of separation between Church and State."[12] Jefferson's words led to the creation of the Establishment Clause (Separation of church and state) that we use today. The Establishment Clause states:

Congress shall make no law respecting an
establishment of religion, or prohibiting the
free exercise thereof: or abridging the freedom
of speech, or of the press; or the right of the

people peaceably to assemble, and to petition the Government for a redress of grievances.[13]

The First Amendment clearly asserts that its intent is not to keep the church out of the state but to keep the state out of the church. Millions of people are clueless about this provision. Even though there is no prohibition to worshiping in the Capitol, I've been told that what I did that night and subsequent nights broke the law. Evidently, singing is viewed as a form of protest and protest within the Capitol itself is not allowed.

After that initial service, the founders asked me if I would return to Washington, DC twice a month to lead worship in these gatherings for members of Congress, staff, and other guests. Since that time, I have spent countless hours on airplanes flying from Los Angeles to Washington, DC, and back as well as countless hours on Capitol Hill.

Steve at the United States Capitol

Since singing that first night in the Capitol, I have sung many times in HC5, the Rotunda, Statuary Hall, and other rooms in the building. The natural reverb of singing in that domed space with marble floors is pretty spectacular. Few people know that the ceiling is so tall that the Statue of Liberty could actually fit in the Rotunda.

Before COVID-19 and the incursion into the Capitol on January 6, 2021, members of Congress often escorted constituents into the Capitol for a late-night tour and history lesson. On more than one occasion, members of Congress have seen me when they were giving tours to their constituents and asked me to sing for their folks. I am always happy to oblige. If either Congressman Jeff Duncan or Congressman Louie Gohmert spots me, it is inevitable that I'll wind up singing "America, the Beautiful" or "How Great Thou Art." I'm glad to sing for any member of Congress regardless of political affiliation. After all, it's the Capitol!

I spend my time on Capitol Hill not only leading worship but also engaging with members of Congress, staff, and United States Capital Police. What I have discovered is that Capitol Hill is a challenging place to work!

Before each trip to Washington, DC, I write over 200 personal notes of encouragement to members of Congress. Once there, I walk approximately ten miles on the hard marble floors of the House and Senate office buildings as well as the Capitol. I've actually gone through several pairs of shoes and my feet always scream at me the morning after, "Give us a break!"

My notes are for members of both political parties as my presence on the Hill is genuinely nonpartisan. Each note contains my handwritten encouragement and a word of scripture such as "The words of the reckless pierce like swords, but the tongue of the wise brings healing" (Prov. 12:18).

One day, I entered the office of a Democrat representative. She had been getting my notes for years, but we had never met face to face. She stood just inside the door, and when I handed her my note, she said, "Oh, you're the one who's been praying for me." Ever since, we've been fast friends. If I see her hurrying to the House Chamber to vote, she'll slow down and let me walk with her.

I've heard it said that everyone has a battle that we know nothing about. This is especially true in the halls of Congress. Allow me to share some experiences I've had while spending time on Capitol Hill.

One evening, I stepped into an elevator in the Capitol. Soon, I was joined by a member of Congress just before the door closed. I had never met this person. With only the two of us in the elevator, I asked, "What do you need God to do for you?"

The congressperson was visibly touched and shared a very personal need. As I began to pray, this individual grabbed hold of my shoulder while the elevator made its way to the sub-basement level. When I finished praying, the person said, "God put you here for me tonight." On my next trip back to Capitol Hill, we spent additional time together. It was a divine appointment.

One afternoon, I visited the office of a member of the House. I had encountered him a couple of times while delivering my notes to congressional offices. After I entered, he closed the door and began to pour out his heart.

"I am so lonely," he said. "I'm lonely here on the Hill, and I'm lonely when I return to the district." Struck by his vulnerability and honesty, I got it! These 535 people who are members of the House and Senate are just like other Americans with family challenges, illnesses, and financial problems. Another divine appointment.

Another night, I stood in the sub-basement of the Capitol where the tram from the Rayburn Office Building ends. A member walked up to me and started singing one of my patriotic songs. We both laughed. I asked him, "What do you need God to do for you?"

The moment turned serious as he shared that his son is a drug addict. He and his wife never know where their son is unless the police call to tell them that he is in custody. Divine appointment.

While walking down the hall of the Longworth Building, I encountered a member of Congress. We chatted briefly and then I asked the question. "What do you need God to do for you?" He said, "My wife and I need our joy back." He then shared that they had experienced a tragic loss in their family. Divine appointment.

As I walked down the hall one afternoon, a representative saw me and said, "Ah, the great encourager." What an encouragement and confirmation! The splendor of music has been a door-opener for divine appointments to the powerful in the halls of Congress, and my words of encouragement have blended with the songs that God has gifted me to sing.

ENCORE

I never could have imagined a ministry on Capitol Hill. My voice was the entrée to encouraging others in government. Let your voice be heard.

Epilogue

What does the future hold? I intend to sing. I intend to look for divine appointments where my singing voice and my speaking voice can plant seeds of encouragement into the lives of others. No song is as sweet as a song of hope.

"Those who wish to sing always find a song."[14]

God made my heart to hold a song
And filled my mouth with hope
To share His never-ending love
With each and every note.
So when my voice has lost its sheen
And lyrics fade away
I still will sing the Father's praise
Until my final day.

Lyrics by Steve Amerson

Notes

1. Hans Christian Andersen, "A Quote by Hans Christian Andersen, *Goodreads,* Accessed May 5, 2021: https://www.goodreads.com/quotes/90636-where-words-fail-music-speaks.

2. Horatius Bonar, "A Quote by Horatius Bonar," *Hymnary.org*, Accessed May 18, 2021: https://hymnary.org/text/love_that_casts_out_fear_o_love_that.

3. Martin Luther, "A Quote by Martin Luther, *Goodreads,* Accessed May 10, 2021: https://www.goodreads.com/quotes/665899-next-to-the-word-of-god-the-noble-art-of.

4. *Canticum Sacrum, Wikipedia,* Accessed May 30, 2021: https://en.wikipedia.org/wiki/Canticum_Sacrum.

5. Plato, "A Quote by Plato," *PassItOn,* Accessed June 7, 2021: https://www.passiton.com/inspirational-quotes/6701-music-gives-a-soul-to-the-universe-wings-to.

6. Steve Amerson and Lowell Alexander, "Because of the Brave," Track #6 on *Steve Amerson Amazed by America,* Steve Amerson Music & 716 Music Publishing, 2009.

7. Orrin Hatch and Phil Naish and Lowell Alexander, "Blades of Grass and Pure White Stones," Sony/ATV Cross Keys Publishing and StarSaylor Music Publishing, 2004.

8. Frank Wildhorn and Nan Knighton, "Into the Fire," *The Scarlet Pimpernel,* WB Music Corp, 1997.

9. Steve Amerson and Lowell Alexander, "This Could Be the Day," Birdwing/Steve Amerson Music, 1994.

10. Steve Amerson and Lowell Alexander, "The Father's Heart," Steve Amerson Music and Bridge Building Music, Inc., 1996.

11. Thomas Jefferson, "Thomas Jefferson to Charles Thomson, 9 January 1816," *Founders Online,* National Archives, https://founders.archives.gov/documents/Jefferson/03-09-02-0216. [Original source: *The Papers of Thomas Jefferson*, Retirement Series, vol. 9, *September 1815 to April 1816*, ed. J. Jefferson Looney. Princeton: Princeton University Press, 2012, pp. 340–342.]

12. Thomas Jefferson, "I. Draft Reply to the Danbury Baptist Association, [on before 3 December 1801]," *Founders*

Online, National Archives, https://founders.archives.gov/documents/Jefferson/01-36-02-0152-0002. [Original source: *The Papers of Thomas Jefferson*, vol. 36, *1 December 1801–3 March 1802*, ed. Barbara B. Oberg. Princeton: Princeton University Press, 2009, pp. 254–256.]

13. United States. Const. Art. II, Sec. 1.

14. Swedish proverb, *PassItOn:* https://www.passiton.com/inspirational-quotes/5129those-who-wish-to-sing-always-find-a-song.

BIBLIOGRAPHY

Amerson, Steve and Lowell Alexander. "Because of
    the Brave." Track #6 on *Steve Amerson Amazed by
    America*. Steve Amerson Music & 716 Music Publishing,
    2009.

Amerson, Steve and Lowell Alexander. "The Father's
    Heart." Steve Amerson Music and Bridge Building
    Music, Inc., 1996.

Amerson, Steve and Lowell Alexander. "This Could Be the
    Day." Birdwing/Steve Amerson Music, 1994.

Andersen, Hans Christian. "A Quote by Hans Christian
    Andersen, *Goodreads*. Accessed May 5, 2021. https://
    www.goodreads.com/quotes/90636-where-words-fail-
    music-speaks.

Bonar, Horatius. "A Quote by Horatius Bonar." *Hymnary.
    org*. Accessed May 18, 2021. https://hymnary.org/text/
    love_that_casts_out_fear_o_love_that.

Canticum Sacrum. *Wikipedia*. Accessed May 30, 2021.
    https://en.wikipedia.org/wiki/Canticum_Sacrum.

Hatch, Orrin and Phil Naish and Lowell Alexander. "Blades of Grass and Pure White Stones." Sony/ATV Cross Keys Publishing and StarSaylor Music Publishing, 2004.

Jefferson, Thomas. "I. Draft Reply to the Danbury Baptist Association, [on or before 31 December 1801]," *Founders Online*. National Archives. https://founders.archives.gov/documents/Jefferson/01-36-02-0152-0002.

[Original source: *The Papers of Thomas Jefferson*, vol. 36, *1 December 1801–3 March 1802*, ed. Barbara B. Oberg. Princeton: Princeton University Press, 2009, pp. 254–256.]

Jefferson, Thomas. "Thomas Jefferson to Charles Thomson, 9 January 1816," *Founders Online*. National Archives. https://founders.archives.gov/documents/Jefferson/03-09-02-0216.

[Original source: *The Papers of Thomas Jefferson*, Retirement Series, vol. 9, *September 1815 to April 1816*, ed. J. Jefferson Looney. Princeton: Princeton University Press, 2012, pp. 340–342.]

Luther, Martin. "A Quote by Martin Luther. *Goodreads*. Accessed May 10, 2021. https://www.goodreads.com/quotes/665899-next-to-the-word-of-god-the-noble-art-of.

Plato. "A Quote by Plato." *PassItOn*. Accessed June 7, 2021. https://www.passiton.com/inspirational-quotes/6701-music-gives-a-soul-to-the-universe-wings-to.

Swedish proverb. *PassItOn:* https://www.passiton.com/inspirational-quotes/5129those-who- wish-to-sing-always-find-a-song.

United States. Const. Art. II, Sec. 1.

Wildhorn, Frank and Nan Knighton. "Into the Fire." *The Scarlet Pimpernel*. WB Music Corp, 1997.

About the Author

Steve Amerson has an established reputation as an excellent tenor with a vocal flexibility that allows him to feel at home in both popular/contemporary music and classical literature. With his wealth and depth of performance experience, Steve is known as *America's Tenor.*

He has been a featured soloist for hundreds of churches and performed with symphonies throughout the United States and abroad, including performances at the Hollywood Bowl and Carnegie Hall.

Steve has ministered alongside well-known pastors and authors, including Billy Graham, Chuck Swindoll, Jack Hayford, and David Jeremiah.

In the Los Angeles studios, he is a sought-after talent. His voice can be heard on 175 feature films and countless television shows, commercials, and video games. His nineteen solo CDs feature sacred, Broadway, patriotic, and Christmas selections.

In 2006, Steve began performing for the Congressional Medal of Honor Foundation and Society events throughout the United States. In 2009, the Medal of Honor Society presented him with the "Bob Hope Award for Excellence in Entertainment." Singing for numerous events in support of those in the military and their families is one of Steve's major commitments.

Since July of 2014, Steve has sung and led worship in Capitol Worship, the first weekly worship services to be held in the United States Capitol in 144 years. Traveling to Washington twice a month, he offers spiritual leadership and encouragement to members of Congress and those who work on Capitol Hill.

Steve and his wife, Kristine, live in Southern California near their two adult children and spouses and five grand-sons.

The Amerson Family

Back Row: Matthew, Vanessa, & Walker, Kat & Dave
Front Row: Hudson, Steve, Judah, Theo, and Kristine.
(Ezra was in Kat's tummy.)

To learn more about Steve and his music, scan the below QR code and visit www.steveamerson.com.